Study Guide

for Bennett and Hess's

Criminal Investigation

Sixth Edition

Christine M. Orthmann

Wadsworth
Thomson Learning

Australia • Canada • Mexico • Singapore • Spain • United Kingdom • United States

For more information, contact
Wadsworth/Thomson Learning
10 Davis Drive
Belmont, CA 94002-3098
USA
http://www.wadsworth.com

International Headquarters
Thomson Learning
International Division
290 Harbor Drive, 2nd Floor
Stamford, CT 06902-7477
USA

UK/Europe/Middle East/South Africa
Thomson Learning
Berkshire House
168-173 High Holborn
London WC1V 7AA
United Kingdom

Asia
Thomson Learning
60 Albert Complex, #15-01
Singapore 189969

Canada
Nelson Thomson Learning
1120 Birchmount Road
Toronto, Ontario M1K 5G4
Canada

ISBN 0-534-57656-7

CONTENTS

Chapter 1

CRIMINAL INVESTIGATION: AN OVERVIEW

_____

CHAPTER 1 QUESTIONS

Answer each question as completely as you can.

1.   What is a criminal investigation?

2.   What are the major goals of criminal investigation?

3.   What basic functions do investigators perform?

4.   What characteristics are important in investigators?

5.   Who usually arrives at the crime scene first?

6.   What should be done initially?

7.   What do you do if a suspect is still at a crime scene? Has recently fled the scene?

8.   How are the crime scene and evidence protected and for how long?

9.   What responsibilities are included in the preliminary investigation?

10.   What is the meaning and importance of *res gestae* statements?

11.   How do you determine whether a crime has been committed?

12.   What basic components are included in an investigative plan?

13.   Who is responsible for solving crimes?

14.   With whom must investigators relate?

15.   How can investigators avoid civil lawsuits?

Check your answers with those that follow.

CHAPTER 1 ANSWERS

1.   A criminal investigation is the process of discovering, collecting, preparing, identifying and presenting evidence to determine what happened and who is responsible.

2.   The goals of criminal investigation are to:
   - Determine whether a crime has been committed.
   - Legally obtain information and evidence to identify the responsible person.
   - Arrest the suspect.
   - Recover stolen property.
   - Present the best possible case to the prosecutor.

3.   Investigators perform the following functions:
   - Provide emergency assistance.
   - Secure the crime scene.
   - Photograph, videotape and sketch.
   - Take notes and write reports.
   - Search for, obtain and process physical evidence.
   - Obtain information from witnesses and suspects.
   - Identify suspects.
   - Conduct raids, surveillances, stakeouts and undercover assignments.
   - Testify in court.

4.   Effective investigators obtain and retain information, apply technical knowledge, remain open minded, objective and logical. Effective investigators are emotionally well balanced, detached, inquisitive, suspecting, discerning, self-disciplined and persevering.

5.   The initial response is usually by a patrol officer assigned to the area where a crime has occurred.

6.   The priorities are as follows:
   - Handle emergencies first.
   - Secure the scene.
   - Investigate.

7.   Any suspect at the scene should be detained, questioned and then released or arrested, depending on circumstances. If a suspect has recently left the scene, obtain a description of the suspect, any vehicles, direction of travel and any items taken. Dispatch the information to headquarters immediately.

8.   Take all necessary measures to secure the crime scene—including locking, roping, barricading and guarding—until the preliminary investigation is completed.

9.   Responsibilities during the preliminary investigation include:
   - Measuring, photographing, videotaping and sketching the scene.
   - Searching for evidence.
   - Identifying, collecting, examining and processing physical evidence.
   - Questioning victims, witnesses and suspects.
   - Recording all statements and observations in notes.

10.   *Res gestae* statements are generally spontaneous statements made at the time of a crime, concerning and closely related to actions involved in the crime. They are often considered more truthful than later, planned responses.

11.   Determine whether a crime has been committed by knowing the elements of each major offense, the evidence that supports them and ascertaining whether they are present. Try to determine when the event occurred.

12.   A written plan contains four basic components—predication, elements to prove, preliminary steps and investigative steps.

13.   The ultimate responsibility for solving crimes lies with all police personnel. It must be a cooperative, coordinated departmental effort.

14.   Investigators interrelate with uniformed police officers, dispatchers, the prosecutor's staff, the defense counsel, supervisors, physicians, the coroner or medical examiner, laboratories and citizens, including victims.

15.   To avoid or minimize lawsuits:
   - Know the law.
   - Know your department's policies.
   - Become the best police officer possible.
   - Develop and fine-tune your policing skills further through education.
   - Sharpen your effectiveness in all aspects of human relations.
   - Officially report understaffing and equipment or vehicle needs malfunctions.
   - Double-check a supervisor's orders and evaluate fellow officers' performance.
   - Unless it is a priority, do not get involved when off duty.

KEY TERMS

Define each term in the space provided.

civil liability

community policing

crime

criminal intent

criminal investigation

criminal statute

criminalistics

elements of the crime

emergency

fact

felony

forensic science

inference

intuition

investigate

misdemeanor

modus operandi (MO)

opinion

ordinance

predication

res gestae statements

Check your definitions by comparing them with those contained in the Glossary.

CHAPTER 1 SUMMARY

Fill in the blanks with the appropriate words and phrases.

A criminal investigation is the process of _____, _____, preparing, identifying and presenting _____ to determine what happened and who is responsible.

The _____ of police investigation vary from department to department, but most investigations aim to:

- Determine whether a _____ has been committed.

- Legally obtain sufficient information and evidence to identify the responsible _____.

- Locate and arrest the _____.

- Recover _____ _____.

- Present the best possible case to the _____.

Among the numerous functions performed by investigators are providing emergency assistance; securing the _____ _____; photographing, videotaping and _____; taking notes and writing _____; searching for, obtaining and processing _____ evidence; obtaining information from _____ and _____; identifying suspects; conducting raids, _____, stakeouts and _____ assignments; and _____ in court.

All investigators whether patrol officers or detectives, are more effective when they possess certain intellectual, _____ and _____ characteristics. Effective investigators obtain and retain _____, apply _____ knowledge, and remain open minded, objective and _____. They are emotionally well balanced,

_____, inquisitive, suspecting, discerning, self-disciplined and _____.

Further, they are _____ _____ and have good _____ and

_____.

   The first officer to arrive at a crime scene is usually a _____ _____

assigned to the area. In any preliminary investigation, it is critical to establish priorities. Handle

_____ first and then _____ the scene. Any suspect at the scene should

be _____, questioned and then either _____ or _____,

depending on circumstances. If a suspect has recently left the scene, obtain a general

_____ of the suspect, any _____, direction of travel and any

_____ taken. Dispatch the information to _____ immediately.

   After emergencies are dealt with, the first and most important function is to protect the

crime scene and _____. Take all necessary measures to secure the crime scene—

including locking, _____, barricading and _____—until the

preliminary investigation is completed.

   Once the scene is secured, proceed with the preliminary investigation which

includes measuring, _____, videotaping and sketching the scene; searching

for _____; identifying, collecting, examining and processing _____

evidence; questioning _____, witnesses and _____; and recording all

statements and observations in _____. _____ _____ statements are

spontaneous statements made at the time of a crime, concerning and closely related to actions

involved in the crime. They are often considered more _____ than later, planned

responses. The crime scene is _____ through these records.

As soon as possible, determine whether a crime has been committed by knowing the elements of each _____ _____ and the evidence that supports them and then ascertaining whether they are present. Also try to determine _____ the event occurred.

A properly formulated written _____ plan is vital and contains four basic components—_____, elements to _____, _____ steps and investigative steps.

Even in police departments that have highly specialized investigation departments, the ultimate responsibility for solving crimes lies with all _____ _____. It must be a cooperative, coordinated _____effort. Cooperation and coordination of efforts is also required outside the police department. Investigators must interrelate not only with uniformed patrol officers but also with _____, the prosecutor's staff, the _____ counsel, physicians, the coroner or _____ examiner, laboratories and citizens, including _____. Criminal investigation is, indeed, a mutual effort.

To avoid or minimize lawsuits, (1) know the _____, (2) know your department's _____, (3) become the best police officer possible, (4) develop and fine-tune your policing skills further through _____, (5) sharpen your effectiveness in all aspects of _____ _____, (6) officially report _____ and equipment or _____ needs and malfunctions, (7) double-check a _____ orders and evaluate fellow officers' performance and (8) unless it is a priority, don't get involved when _____ _____.

Check your answers by comparing them with the summary of Chapter 1 in your text.

Chapter 2

INVESTIGATIVE PHOTOGRAPHY AND CRIME-SCENE SKETCHES

CHAPTER 2 QUESTIONS

Answer each question as completely as you can.

1.   What purposes are served by crime-scene photography?

2.   What are the advantages and disadvantages of using photography?

3.   What is the minimum photographic equipment for an investigator?

4.   What errors in technique must be avoided?

5.   What should be photographed at a crime scene and in what sequence?

6.   What types of photography are used in criminal investigations?

7.   What basic rules of evidence must photographs meet?

8.   What purposes are served by the crime-scene sketch?

9.   What should be sketched?

10.   What materials are needed to make a rough sketch?

11.   What steps are taken in making a rough sketch?

12.   How are plotting methods used in sketches?

13.   When is a sketch or a scale drawing admissible in court?

Check your answers with those that follow.

CHAPTER 2 ANSWERS

1.   Photographs and videotapes reproduce the crime scene in detail for presentation to the prosecution, defense, witnesses, judge and jury in court. They are used in investigating, prosecuting and police training.

2.   Advantages of photographs are that they can be taken immediately, they accurately represent the crime scene and evidence, they create interest and they increase attention to testimony. Disadvantages of photographs are that they are not selective, they do not show actual distances and may be distorted and they may be damaged by mechanical errors in shooting or processing.

3.   At a minimum, have available and be skilled in operating a 35 mm camera, an instant-print camera, a press camera, a fingerprint camera and video equipment.

4.   Take photographs before anything is disturbed. Avoid inaccuracies and distortions.

5.   First photograph the general area, then specific areas and finally specific objects of evidence. Take exterior shots first because they are the most subject to alteration by weather and security violations.

6.   Types of investigative photography include crime-scene, surveillance, aerial, night, laboratory, lineup and mug-shot photography.

7.   Photographs must be material, relevant, competent, accurate, free of distortion and noninflammatory.

8.   A crime-scene sketch assists in (1) interviewing and interrogating people, (2) preparing the investigative report and (3) presenting the case in court.

9.   Sketch all serious crime and accident scenes after photographs are taken and before anything is moved. Sketch the entire scene, the objects and the evidence.

10.   Materials for the rough sketch include paper, pencil, long steel measuring tape, carpenter-type ruler, straightedge, clipboard, eraser, compass, protractor and thumbtacks.

11.   To sketch a crime scene:
      ▪ Observe and plan.
      ▪ Measure distances.
      ▪ Outline the area.
      ▪ Locate objects and evidence within the outline.
      ▪ Record details.
      ▪ Make notes.
      ▪ Identify the sketch with a legend and a scale.
      ▪ Reassess the sketch.

12.   Plotting methods are used to locate objects and evidence on the sketch. They include the use of rectangular coordinates, a baseline, triangulation and compass points.

13.   An admissible sketch is one drawn or personally witnessed by an investigator that accurately portrays a crime scene. A scale drawing also is admissible if the investigating officer drew it or approved it after it was drawn and if it accurately represents the rough sketch. The rough sketch must remain available as evidence.

KEY TERMS

Define each term in the space provided.

backing

baseline method

compass point method

competent photograph

cross-projection sketch

finished scale drawing

laser-beam photography

legend

macrophotography

marker

material photograph

microphotography

mug shots

overlapping

plotting methods

rectangular-coordinate method

relevant photograph

rogues' gallery

rough sketch

scale

sketch

trap photography

triangulation

ultraviolet-light photography

Check your definitions by comparing them with those contained in the Glossary.

CHAPTER 2 SUMMARY

Fill in the blanks with the appropriate words and phrases.

_____, one of the first investigative techniques to be used at a crime scene,

helps to establish that a crime was committed and to trace the occurrence of the crime.

Photographs and videotapes reproduce the crime scene in detail for presentation to the

_____, defense, _____, judge and jury in court. They are used in

_____, prosecution and _____ training.

Photography has become increasingly important in criminal investigation because it can

_____ _____ evidence, accurately represent the _____

- _____ and evidence, create _____ and increase attention to testimony.

However, photographs also have disadvantages: they are not _____, do not show actual _____ and may be _____ and damaged by _____

errors in shooting or processing.

At a minimum, have available and be skilled in operating a _____, an

instant-print camera, a _____ camera, a _____ camera and

_____ equipment. Take photographs of the entire crime scene before anything is

disturbed and avoid _____ and _____. First photograph the

_____ area, then _____ areas and finally specific _____

of evidence. Take _____ shots first. Investigative photography includes crime-

scene surveillance, _____, _____, laboratory, mug shot and _____.

After photographs are taken, they must be properly _____ , filed and kept

_____ to be admissible as evidence. In addition, rules of evidence dictate that photographs

be _____, _____, competent, _____, free of distortion and

_____.

In addition to photographs, crime-scene _____ are often used. A crime-

scene sketch assists in (1) _____ and interrogating people, (2) preparing the

_____ _____ and (3) presenting the case in _____. Photographs,

sketches and _____ _____ are often needed to provide a clear picture of the

scene.

Sketch the scene of a serious crime or accident after _____ it and before

_____ anything. Include all relevant _____ and _____. Materials needed

for making the rough sketch include paper, pencil, long steel _____ _____,

carpenter-type ruler, _____, clipboard, eraser, _____, protractor and

thumbtacks. The steps involved in sketching include (1) observing and _____;

(2) measuring distances and _____ the general area; (3) locating, _____ and recording objects and evidence within the outline; (4) taking _____; (5) identifying the _____; and (6) reassessing the _____.

Plotting methods useful in locating objects and evidence include _____ coordinate, baseline, _____ and _____ point. A _____- _____ sketch shows the floor and walls in the same plane.

After completing the sketch, record in your notes the _____ conditions, colors, _____ present at the scene and all other information that cannot be _____. Then place a _____ in the lower corner of the sketch, _____ the room or area outline. Identify the scene completely—the location, type of _____ and case _____. Include the _____ and an _____ indicating north pointing to the top of the sketch. Include the _____ of the person making the sketch. Before leaving the scene, make sure nothing has been _____. Keep the sketch _____ because it is the basis for the finished scale drawing and may be needed as _____ in court.

The finished scale drawing is done in _____ on a good grade of paper and is drawn to scale using _____ _____. Both the _____ sketch and the _____ drawing are admissible in court if they are made or personally witnessed by the _____ and accurately portray the _____ _____. The original rough sketch must remain available as evidence.

Check your answers by comparing them with the summary of Chapter 2 in your text.

Chapter 3

INVESTIGATIVE NOTES AND REPORTS

_____

CHAPTER 3 QUESTIONS

Answer each question as completely as you can.

1.   Why are notes important in an investigation?

2.   When should notes be taken?

3.   What should be recorded in investigative notes?

4.   How are notes recorded?

5.   What are the characteristics of effective notes?

6.   If they are retained, where should notes be filed?

7.   How are notes used in court and what problems can arise?

8.   What steps are involved in writing an investigative report?

9.   What types of investigative reports may be required?

10.   Why are reports important to an investigation?

11.   How should the narrative be structured?

12.   What are the characteristics of effective investigative reports?

Check your answers with those that follow.

CHAPTER 3 ANSWERS

1.   Investigative notes are a permanent written record of the facts of a case to be used in further investigation, in writing reports and in prosecuting the case.

2.   Start to take notes as soon as possible after receiving a call to respond and continue recording information as it is received throughout the investigation.

3.   Record all information that helps to answer the questions: Who? What? Where? When? How? and Why?

4.   Write brief, legible, abbreviated notes that others can understand.

5.   Effective notes are complete, accurate, specific, factual, clear, well organized and legible.

6.   If notes are retained, file them in a secure location readily accessible to investigators.

7.   Original notes are legally admissible in court, and officers may use them to refresh their memories. Officers should take to court only those notes that pertain to the particular case.

8.   Steps in report writing:
     1.   Gather the facts: Investigate, interview, interrogate.
     2.   Record the facts immediately.
     3.   Organize the facts.
     4.   Write the report.
     5.   Evaluate the report: Edit and proofread; revise if necessary.

9.   Investigators usually complete (1) an initial or preliminary report, (2) supplemental or progress reports and (3) a closing or final report.

10.   Reports are a permanent written record of important facts that can be used to examine the past, keep other police officers informed, continue investigations, prepare court cases, provide the court with relevant facts, coordinate law enforcement activities, plan for future law enforcement services and evaluate law enforcement officers' performance.

11.   Usually the narrative is structured as follows:
      1.   The opening paragraph of a police report states the time, date, type of incident and how you became involved.
      2.   The next paragraph contains what you were told by the victim or witnesses. For each person talked to, use a separate paragraph.
      3.   Next record what you did based on the information you received.
      4.   The final paragraph states the disposition of the case.

12.   An effective report uses paragraphs, the past tense, first person and active voice. It is factual, accurate, objective, complete, concise, clear, mechanically correct, written in standard English, legible and reader focused.

KEY TERMS

Define each term in the space provided.

active voice ✔

best evidence

chronological order ✔

conclusionary language ✔

first person ✔

narrative ✔

past tense ✔

template

Check your definitions by comparing them with those contained in the Glossary.

CHAPTER 3 SUMMARY

Fill in the blanks with the appropriate words and phrases.

Investigative _____ and _____ are critical parts of a criminal investigation. Notes are a _____ written record of the facts of a case to be used in further _____, in writing reports and in _____ the case. Start to take notes as soon as possible after receiving an _____ _____ to respond, and continue recording information as it is received throughout the _____.

Record all relevant information concerning the _____, the _____ _____ and the investigation, including information that helps answer the questions: _____? _____? _____? _____? _____? and _____? Write brief, _____ notes that others can understand. Make them complete, _____, specific, _____, clear, well organized and _____. After you have written your report, file your notes in a _____ location readily accessible to you or _____ them according to department policy. Original notes are _____ _____ in court and may be used to _____ from or to refresh your memory. Take to court only those notes that pertain to the _____.

Good notes are the foundation for effective reports. The five steps in writing a report are to (1) gather _____, (2) take _____, (3) _____ the notes, (4) write the report and (5) _____ it. Investigators usually complete an initial or _____ report, _____ or progress report and a _____ or final report. These provide a permanent written record of important facts that can be used to examine the _____, keep other _____ _____ informed, continue _____, prepare court cases, provide the court with _____ facts,

_____ law enforcement activities, plan for future law enforcement services and

_____ law enforcement officers' performance.

A police report's narrative might be structured as follows:

- The opening paragraph of a police report states the _____, _____, _____ of incident and how you became involved.

- The next paragraph contains what you were told by the _____ or _____. For each person you talked to, use a separate _____.

- Next, record what you did based on the _____ you received.

- The final paragraph states the _____ of the case.

An effective report uses _____, the _____ tense, _____ person and _____ voice. It is factual, accurate, _____, complete, _____, clear, _____ correct, written in _____ English, legible and _____ focused.

Check your answers by comparing them with the summary of Chapter 3 in your text.

Chapter 4

SEARCHES

_____

CHAPTER 4 QUESTIONS

Answer each question as completely as you can.

1.　　Which constitutional amendment restricts investigative searches?

2.　　What is required for an effective search?

3.　　What are the preconditions and limitations of a legal search?

4.　　When is a warrantless search justified?

5.　　What basic restriction is placed on all searches?

6.   What precedents are established by the *Carroll, Chambers, Chimel, Mapp, Terry* and
      Weeks decisions?

7.   What are the characteristics of a successful crime-scene search?

8.   What is included in organizing a crime-scene search?

9.   What is physical evidence?

10.   What search patterns are used in exterior searches? Interior searches?

11.   What is plain-view evidence?

12.   How do investigators search a vehicle, a suspect and a dead body?

13.   How can dogs be used in searches?

14.   What is the exclusionary rule and how does it affect investigators?

15.   What are the fruit-of-the-poisonous-tree doctrine, the inevitable-discovery doctrine and the good-faith doctrine?

Check your answers with those that follow.

CHAPTER 4 ANSWERS

1.   The Fourth Amendment to the U.S. Constitution forbids unreasonable searches and seizures.

2.   To conduct an effective search, know the legal requirements for searching, the items being searched for and the elements of the crime being investigated; be organized, systematic and thorough.

3.   A search can be justified and therefore considered legal if any of the following conditions are met:
- A search warrant has been issued.
- Consent is given.
- The search is incidental to a lawful arrest.
- An emergency exists.

A search conducted with a warrant must be limited to the specific area and specific items named in the warrant. Consent to search must be voluntary, and the search must be limited to the area for which consent is given.

4.   A warrantless search in the absence of a lawful arrest or consent is justified only in emergencies where probable cause exists and the search must be conducted immediately.

5.   The most important limitation on any search is that the scope must be narrowed. General searches are unconstitutional.

6.   The *Carroll* decision established that automobiles may be searched without a warrant if (1) there is probable cause for the search and (2) the vehicle would be gone before a search warrant could be obtained.

Chambers v Maroney (1970) established that a vehicle may be taken to headquarters to be searched.

The *Chimel* decision established that a search incidental to a lawful arrest must be made simultaneously with the arrest and must be confined to the area within the suspect's immediate control.

The *Terry* decision established that a patdown or frisk is a "protective search for weapons" and as such must be "confined to a scope reasonable designed to discover guns, knives, clubs, and other hidden instruments for the assault of a police officer or others."

Weeks v United States (1914) made the exclusionary rule applicable at the federal level; *Mapp v Ohio* (1961) made it applicable to *all* courts.

7.   A successful crime-scene search locates, identifies and preserves all evidence present.

8.   Organizing a search includes dividing the duties, selecting a search pattern, assigning personnel and equipment and giving instructions.

9.   Knowing what to search for is indispensable to an effective crime-scene search. Evidence is anything material and relevant to the crime being investigated.

10.   Exterior search patterns divide an area into lanes, concentric circles or zones. Interior search go from the general to the specific, usually in a circular pattern, covering all surfaces of a search area. The floor should be searched first.

11.   Plain-view evidence—unconcealed evidence seen by an officer engaged in a lawful activity—is admissible in court.

12.   In vehicle searches, remove occupants from the car. First search the area around the vehicle and then the exterior. Finally, search the interior along one side from front to back, and then return along the other side to the front. In suspect searches, if the suspect has not been arrested, confine your search to a patdown or frisk for weapons. If the suspect has been arrested, make a complete body search for weapons and evidence. In either event, always be on your guard. Search a dead body systematically and completely. Include the immediate area around and under the body.

13.   Dogs can be trained to locate suspects, narcotics and explosives.

14.   The exclusionary rule established that courts may not accept evidence obtained by unreasonable search and seizure, regardless of its relevance to a case.

15.   The fruit-of-the-poisonous-tree doctrine established that evidence obtained as a result of an earlier illegality must be excluded from trial. The inevitable-discovery doctrine established that if illegally obtained evidence would in all likelihood eventually have been discovered legally, it may be used. The good-faith doctrine established that illegally obtained evidence may be admissible if the police were truly not aware they were violating a suspect's Fourth Amendment rights.

KEY TERMS

Define each term in the space provided.

Carroll decision

certiorari

Chimel decision

circle search

curtilage

"elephant-in-a-matchbox" doctrine

exclusionary rule

frisk

fruit-of-the-poisonous-tree doctrine

good-faith doctrine

grid

immediate control

inevitable-discovery doctrine

lane

lane search pattern

mobility

no-knock warrant

patdown

plain-view evidence

probable cause

protective sweep

search

search patterns

sector

strip-search pattern

true scene

uncontaminated scene

zone

Check your definitions by comparing them with those contained in the Glossary.

CHAPTER 4 SUMMARY

Fill in the blanks with the appropriate words and phrases.

The _____ Amendment to the Constitution forbids _____searches and

seizures. Therefore, investigators must know what constitutes a _____,

_____ search. To search effectively, know the legal requirements for searching, the

_____ you are searching for and the _____ of the crime. Be _____,

_____ and thorough.

A search can be justified if (1) a _____ _____ has been issued,

(2) _____ is given, (3) the search is _____ to a lawful _____ or

(4) an _____ exists. Each of these four situations has limitations. A search conducted

with a warrant must be limited to the _____ and _____ specified in the warrant. A

search conducted with consent requires that the consent be _____ and that the

search be limited to the _____ for which the consent was given. A search incidental to

a lawful arrest must be made _____ with the arrest and be confined to the area

within the suspect's _____ _____ *(Chimel)*. A _____

search in the absence of a lawful arrest or consent is justified only in _____

where _____ _____ exists and the search must be conducted immediately.

       The most important limitation on any search is that the _____ must be

narrowed; _____ searches are unconstitutional. However, _____-

_____ evidence—unconcealed evidence seen by an officer engaged in a lawful

activity—may be seized and <u>is/is not</u> admissible in court.

       A successful crime-scene search _____, _____ and _____ all

evidence present. For maximum effectiveness, a search must be well _____.

This entails _____ the duties, selecting a search _____, assigning

personnel and equipment and giving _____. Knowing _____ to search for

is indispensable to an effective search. Anything _____ and _____ to the crime

might be evidence.

       Search patterns have been developed that help to ensure a thorough search.

_____ search patterns divide an area into lanes, strips, concentric circles or

_____. _____ searches go from the general to the specific, usually in a

_____ pattern that covers all surfaces of the area being searched. The _____

is searched first.

       In addition to crime scenes, investigators frequently search _____,

_____ and _____ _____. When searching a vehicle, _____

the occupants from the car. First search the area _____ the vehicle, then the vehicle's

_____. Finally, search the _____ along one side from front to back and then

return along the other side to the front. Vehicles may be searched without a warrant if there is

_____ _____ and if the vehicle would be _____ before a search warrant could be obtained *(Carroll)*. *Chambers v Maroney* established that a vehicle may be

taken to _____ to be searched in certain circumstances.

When searching a _____ who has not been arrested, confine the search to a

_____ for weapons *(Terry)*. The *Terry* decision established that a _____ or

_____ is a "protective search for weapons" and as such must be "confined to a scope

_____ designed to discover guns, _____, clubs, and other _____

instruments for the assault of a police officer or others." If the suspect has been arrested,

conduct a _____ _____ _____ for weapons and evidence. Always be on

your _____.

Search a dead body systematically and completely; include the immediate area

_____ and _____ the body. Specially trained _____ can be very

helpful in locating suspects, _____ or _____.

If a search is not conducted legally, the evidence obtained is _____.

According to the _____ _____, evidence obtained in unreasonable search

and seizure, regardless of how relevant the evidence may be, is _____ in court.

Weeks v United States established the _____ _____ at the federal level;

Mapp v Ohio made it applicable to all courts.

The fruit-of-the-poisonous-tree doctrine established that evidence obtained as a result of

an _____ _____ must be excluded from trial. Two important

exceptions to the exclusionary rule are the _____-_____ doctrine and the

_____-_____ doctrine. The _____-_____ doctrine states

that if the illegally obtained evidence would in all likelihood eventually have been discovered

anyway, it may be used. The _____-_____ doctrine states that illegally obtained evidence may be admitted into trial if the police were truly unaware that they were violating the

suspect's _____ Amendment rights.

Check your answers by comparing them with the summary of Chapter 4 in your text.

Chapter 5

PHYSICAL EVIDENCE

_____

CHAPTER 5 QUESTIONS

Answer each question as completely as you can.

1.   What is involved in processing physical evidence?

2.   How do investigators determine what evidence is?

3.   What is a standard of comparison and how is it used?

4.   What are common errors in collecting evidence?

5.   How do investigators identify evidence?

6.   What should be recorded in your notes?

7.   How is evidence packaged?

8.   How is evidence conveyed to a department or a laboratory?

9.   What types of evidence are most commonly found in criminal investigations and how are they collected, identified and packaged?

10.   What can and cannot be determined from fingerprints, bloodstains and hairs?

11.   What constitutes "best evidence"?

12.   What is DNA profiling?

13.   How and where is evidence stored?

14.   How is admissibility of physical evidence ensured in court?

15.   How is physical evidence finally disposed of?

Check your answers with those that follow.

CHAPTER 5 ANSWERS

1.   Processing physical evidence includes discovering, recognizing and examining it; collecting, recording and identifying it; packaging, conveying and storing it; exhibiting it in court; and disposing of it when the case is closed.

2.   To determine what is evidence, first consider the apparent crime. Then look for any objects unrelated or foreign to the scene, unusual in location or number, damaged or broken or whose relation to other objects suggests a pattern that fits the crime.

3.   A standard of comparison is an object, measure or model with which evidence is compared to determine whether both came from the same source.

4.   Common errors in collecting evidence are (1) not collecting enough of the sample, (2) not obtaining standards of comparison and (3) not maintaining the integrity of the evidence.

5.   Mark or identify each item of evidence in a way that can be recognized later. Indicate the date and case number as well as your personal identifying mark or initials.

6.   Record in your notes the date and time of collection, where the evidence was found and by whom, the case number, a description of the item and who took custody.

7.   Package each item separately in a durable container to maintain the integrity of evidence.

8.   Personal delivery, registered mail, insured parcel post, air express, Federal Express and United Parcel Service are legal ways to transport evidence. Always specify that the person receiving the evidence is to sign for it.

9.   Frequently examined physical evidence includes fingerprints, voiceprints, shoe and tire impressions, bite marks, tools and toolmarks, weapons and ammunition, glass, soils and minerals, body fluids (including blood), hairs and fibers, safe insulation, rope and tape, drugs, documents and laundry and dry-cleaning marks.

    Any hard, smooth, nonporous surface can contain latent fingerprints. Do not powder a print unless it is necessary, and do not powder a visible print until after you photograph it. Prints of persons with reason to be at the scene are taken and used as elimination prints.

    Cast shoe or tire tread impressions found in dirt, sand or snow.

    Identify each suspect tool with a string tag. Wrap it separately and pack it in a strong box for sending to the laboratory. Photograph toolmarks and then either cast them or send the object on which they appear to a laboratory. A toolmark is compared with a standard of comparison impression rather than with the tool itself.

Examine weapons for latent fingerprints. Photograph weapons and then identify them with a string tag. Unload guns. Record the serial number on the string tag and in your notes. Label the packing container "Firearms." Identify bullets on the base, cartridges on the outside of the case near the bullet end and cartridge cases on the inside near the open end. Put ammunition in cotton or soft paper and ship to a laboratory. Never send live ammunition through the mail; use a common carrier.

Label glass fragments using adhesive tape on each piece. Wrap each piece separately in cotton to avoid chipping and place in a strong box marked "fragile" to send to a laboratory.

Put one pound of comparison soil into a container identified on the outside. Collect evidence soil the same way. Seal both containers to prevent loss, wrap them and send them to a laboratory.

Put samples of safe insulation in paper containers identified on the outside.

Put labeled rope, twine and string into a container. Put tapes on waxed paper or cellophane and then place them in a container.

Put liquid drugs in a bottle and attach a label. Put powdered and solid drugs in a pill or powder box and identify in the same way.

Do not touch documents with your bare hands. Place documents in a cellophane envelope and then in a manila envelope identified on the outside.

Use ultraviolet light to detect invisible laundry marks. Submit the entire garment to a laboratory, identified with a string tag or directly on the garment.

10.   Fingerprints are positive evidence of a person's identity. They cannot, however, indicate a person's age, sex or race.

Blood can be identified as animal or human and is most useful in eliminating suspects. Age, race or sex cannot be determined from blood samples, but DNA analysis can provide positive identification.

Microscopic examination determines whether hair is animal or human. Many characteristics can be determined from human hair: the part of the body it came from; whether it was bleached or dyed, freshly cut, pulled out or burned; and whether there is blood or semen on it. Race, sex and age cannot be determined.

11.   The best-evidence rule stipulates that the original evidence is to be presented whenever possible.

12.   DNA profiling uses material from which chromosomes are made to identify individuals positively. Except for identical twins, no two individuals have the same DNA structure.

13.   Package evidence properly to keep it in substantially the same condition in which it was found. Document custody of the evidence at every stage.

14.   Be able to (1) identify the evidence as that found at the crime scene, (2) describe exactly where it was found, (3) establish its custody from discovery to the present and (4) voluntarily explain any changes that have occurred in the evidence.

15.   Evidence is either returned to the owner, auctioned or destroyed.

KEY TERMS

Define each term in the space provided.

associative evidence

automated fingerprint identification system (AFIS)

barcodes

biometrics

cast

chain of evidence

circumstantial evidence

class characteristics

competent evidence

corpus delicti

corpus delicti evidence

cross-contamination

direct evidence

DNA

DNA profiling

elimination prints

evidence

exculpatory evidence

genetic fingerprint

identifying features

individual characteristics

inkless fingerprints

integrity of evidence

invisible fingerprints

latent fingerprints

material evidence

physical evidence

plastic fingerprints

prima facie evidence

probative evidence

processing evidence

relevant evidence

spectrographic analysis

standard of comparison

toolmark

trace evidence

ultraviolet light

visible fingerprints

voiceprint

X-ray diffraction

Check your definitions by comparing them with those contained in the Glossary.

CHAPTER 5 SUMMARY

Fill in the blanks with the appropriate words and phrases.

Criminal investigations rely heavily upon various types of _____. To be of value, evidence must be _____ and properly seized and _____. Processing physical evidence includes _____, recognizing and _____ it; collecting, _____ and identifying it; _____, conveying and storing it; _____ it in court; and _____ of it when the case is closed. The relative importance of physical evidence depends on its ability to establish that a crime was committed as well as _____, _____ and by whom.

To determine what is evidence, first consider the _____ crime. Then look for any objects _____ or _____ to the scene, unusual in their _____ or _____, damaged or broken or whose relation to other objects suggests a _____ that fits the crime. The more _____ the evidence, the greater its value.

Often _____ of _____ are required. A standard of comparison is an _____, _____ or _____ with which evidence is compared to determine whether both came from the same source. Common errors in collecting evidence are (1) not collecting _____ of the sample, (2) not obtaining _____ of _____ and (3) not maintaining the _____ of the evidence.

Mark or _____ each item of evidence in a way that can be recognized later. Include the _____ and _____ _____ as well as your identifying mark or initials. Record in your notes the date and time of _____, _____ it was found and by whom, case number, _____ of the item and who took custody of it. Package each item _____ in durable containers to maintain the _____ of evidence. Personal delivery, _____ mail,

_____ parcel post, air express, _____ Express and United Parcel Service

(UPS) are legal ways to transport evidence. Always specify that the person who receives the

evidence is to _____ for it.

Frequently examined physical evidence includes fingerprints, _____,

shoe and tire impressions, _____ marks, tools and _____, weapons

and _____, glass, soils and minerals, body fluids (including _____),

hairs and fibers, safe insulation, rope and tape, _____, documents and _____

and dry-cleaning marks.

Know how to locate, develop, photograph, lift and submit _____ for

classification by experts. Any hard, smooth, nonporous surface can contain _____

fingerprints. Do not _____ a print unless it is necessary; do not _____ a

visible print until after _____ it. Prints of persons with reason to be at the

scene are taken and used as _____ prints. Fingerprints are positive evidence

of a person's _____. They cannot, however, indicate a person's _____, _____

or _____.

Cast _____ or _____ _____ impressions found in dirt, sand or

snow. Identify each suspected tool with a _____ tag, wrap it _____,

and pack it in a strong box to send to a _____. Photograph _____

and then either cast them or send the object on which they appear to a laboratory. A toolmark

is compared with a _____ of _____ impression rather than with the tool

itself.

Examine weapons for _____- fingerprints. Photograph _____ and then identify them with a string tag. Unload guns and record their _____ _____ on a string tag and in your notes. Label the packing container "_____." Identify bullets on the _____, cartridges on the _____ of the case near the _____ end and cartridge cases on the _____ near the _____ end. Put _____ in cotton or soft paper and ship to a laboratory. Never send live ammunition through the mail; use a _____ _____ instead.

Label _____ fragments using adhesive tape on each piece. Wrap each piece separately in _____ to avoid _____ and place in a strong box marked "_____" to send to a laboratory. Put one _____ of comparison soil into a container identified on the outside. Collect evidence _____ the same way. Seal both containers to prevent _____, wrap them and send them to a laboratory.

Put samples of safe insulation in _____ containers identified on the outside. Put labeled rope, twine and string in a _____. Put tapes on _____ paper or _____ and then place them in a container. Put _____ _____ in a bottle and attach a label. Put _____ and _____ drugs in a pill or powder box and identify the same way.

Do not touch _____ with your bare hands. Place them in a cellophane envelope and then in a manila envelope identified on the _____. Use _____ light to detect invisible _____ marks. Submit the _____ garment to a laboratory, identified with a string tag or directly on the garment.

_____ can be identified as animal or human and is very useful in eliminating suspects. Age, race or sex can/cannot be determined from blood samples. ____

analysis, however, can provide positive identification. _____ profiling uses material

from which _____ are made to positively identify individuals. Except

for _____ _____, no two individuals have the same DNA structure.

Microscopic examination determines whether _____ is animal or human. Many

characteristics can be determined from human _____: the part of the body it came

from; whether it was bleached or dyed, freshly cut, pulled out or _____; and whether

there is _____ or _____ on it. Race, sex and age can/cannot be determined.

_____ evidence properly to keep it in substantially the same condition

in which it was found. Document custody of the evidence at _____ stage. The _____-

_____ rule stipulates that the original evidence is to be presented in court whenever

possible.

When presenting evidence in court, be able to (1) _____ the evidence as

that found at the crime scene, (2) describe exactly where it was _____, (3) establish

its _____- from discovery to the present and (4) voluntarily explain any _____

that have occurred in the evidence.

After a case is closed, evidence is returned to the owner, _____ or _____.

Check your answers by comparing them with the summary of Chapter 5 in your text.

Chapter 6

OBTAINING INFORMATION

_____

CHAPTER 6 QUESTIONS

Answer each question as completely as you can.

1.   What sources of information are available to investigators?

2.   What is a sources of information file and what does it contain?

3.   What are the goals of interviewing and interrogation?

4.   When and in what order are individuals interviewed?

5.   What two requirements are needed to obtain information?

6.   What is the difference between direct and indirect questions and when is each used?

7.   What technique is likely to assist recall as well as uncover lies?

8.   What basic approaches are used in questioning reluctant interviewees?

9.   What are the characteristics of an effective interviewer or interrogator?

10.   How can communication be improved?

11.   What are the emotional barriers to communication?

12.   What is the Miranda warning and when is it given?

13.   What are the two requirements of a place for conducting interrogations?

14.   What techniques are used in an interrogation?

15.   What are third-degree tactics and what is their place in interrogation?

16.   What restrictions are placed on obtaining a confession?

17.   What significance does a confession have in an investigation?

18.   What should be considered when questioning a juvenile?

19.   What is a polygraph, what is its role in investigation and what is the acceptability of its results in court?

Check your answers with those that follow.

CHAPTER 6 ANSWERS

1.   Important sources of information include (1) reports and records, including those found on the Internet, (2) persons who are not suspects in a crime but who know something about the crime or those involved and (3) suspects in the crime.

2.   A sources of information file contains the name and location of people, organizations and records that may assist in a criminal investigation.

3.   The ultimate goals of interviewing and interrogating are to identify those responsible for a crime and to eliminate the innocent from suspicion.

4.   Interview witnesses separately if possible. Interview the victim or complainant first, then eyewitnesses and then people who did not actually see the crime but who have relevant information.

5.   Two basic requirements to obtain information are to listen and to observe.

6.   Ask direct questions, that is, questions that come right to the point. Use indirect questions—those that skirt the basic question—sparingly.

7.   Repetition is the best way to obtain and to uncover lies.

8.   Appeal to a reluctant interviewee's reason or emotions.

9.   An effective interviewer/interrogator is adaptable, self-controlled, patient, confident, optimistic, objective, sensitive to individual rights and aware of the elements of crimes.

10.   To improve communication: prepare in advance, obtain the information as soon after the incident as possible, be considerate and friendly, use a private setting, eliminate physical barriers, sit rather than stand, encourage conversation, ask simple questions one at a time, listen and observe.

11.   Emotional barriers to communication include ingrained attitudes and prejudices, fear, anger and self-preservation.

12.   The Miranda warning informs suspects of their rights. Give the Miranda warning to every suspect you interrogate.

13.   Conduct interrogations in a place that is private and free from interruptions.

14.   Interrogation techniques include inquiring directly or indirectly, forcing responses, deflating or inflating the ego, minimizing or maximizing crime, projecting the blame, rationalizing and combining approaches.

15.   Third-degree tactics—physical force, threats of force or other physical, mental or psychological abuse—are illegal. Any information so obtained, including confessions, is inadmissible in court.

16.   A confession, oral or handwritten, must be given of the suspect's free will and not in response to fear, threats, promises or rewards.

17.   A confession is only one part of an investigation. Corroborate it by independent evidence.

18.   Obtain parental permission before questioning a youth. Do not use a youth as an informant unless the parents know the situation.

19.   The polygraph scientifically measures respiration and depth of breathing, changes in the skin's electrical resistance and blood pressure and pulse.

KEY TERMS

Define each term in the space provided.

admission

cognitive interview

complainant

confession

custodial arrest

custodial interrogation

direct question

field interview

hypnosis

in custody

indirect question

informant

information age

interrogation

interview

Miranda warning

network

nonverbal communication

polygraph

public safety exception

rapport

sources of information file

statement

suspect

third degree

truth serums

victim

waiver

witness

Check your definitions by comparing them with those contained in the Glossary.

CHAPTER 6 SUMMARY

Fill in the blanks with the appropriate words and phrases.

Most solved cases rely on both _____ evidence and _____ obtained

from a variety of sources. Important sources of information include (1) reports and records,

including those found on the _____, (2) _____ who are not suspects in

the crime but who know something about the crime or those involved and (3) _____

in the crime. A _____-of-_____ file contains the name and location of

people, organizations and records that may assist in a criminal investigation.

The ultimate goals of interviewing and interrogating are to _____ those

responsible for a crime and to eliminate the _____ from suspicion. Interview

anyone other than a suspect who has information about the case. This includes _____,

_____, _____ and _____.

Interview witnesses _____ if possible. Interview the _____ or

complainant first, then _____- and then those who did not actually see the crime

but who have relevant information.

Two basic requirements to obtain information are to _____ and to _____.

Ask _____ questions that come right to the point. Use _____ questions—

those that skirt the basic question—sparingly. _____ is the best way to obtain

recall and to uncover lies. Appeal to a reluctant interviewee's _____ or _____.

     The effective interviewer/interrogator is _____, self-controlled, patient,

confident, _____, objective, sensitive to individual rights and knowledgeable about

the _____ of the crime. Regardless of whether you are interviewing or

interrogating, there are several ways to improve communication: _____ in advance

and obtain the information as soon after the incident as possible; be _____ and

friendly; use a _____ setting and eliminate _____ barriers; _____ rather

than _____; encourage conversation; ask _____ questions one at a time;

listen and _____. Emotional barriers to communication include ingrained attitudes

and _____, _____, _____ or hostility and self-preservation.

     Although many of the same principles apply to interrogating and interviewing,

interrogating involves some special considerations. One important consideration is when to

give the _____ _____ which informs suspects of their rights and must be

given to _____ suspect who is interrogated. It is also important to conduct

interrogations in a place that is _____ and free from _____. Interrogation

techniques include inquiring directly or indirectly, _____ responses, deflating or

inflating the _____, minimizing or maximizing the _____, projecting the

_____, rationalizing and combining approaches. _____-_____

tactics—physical force, threats of force or other physical, mental or psychological abuse—are

illegal. Any information so obtained, including confessions, is _____ in

court. Any confession, oral or handwritten, must be given of the suspect's _____

_____ and not in response to fear, threats, promises or rewards. A confession is

only one part of the investigation. It must be corroborated by _____ evidence.

Special considerations are also observed when questioning _____. Obtain

_____ permission before questioning a juvenile. Do not use a juvenile as an

_____ unless the parents know the situation.

In addition to skills in interviewing and interrogating, you can sometimes use scientific

aids to obtain information and determine its truthfulness. The _____ scientifically

measures respiration and depth of breathing, changes in the skin's electrical resistance and

blood pressure and pulse rate. It is an instrument used to _____ the truth, not a

_____ for investigating and questioning. Although the results are not

presently admissible in court, any _____ obtained as a result of a polygraph

test is admissible. Other scientific aids include _____ and truth _____, but such

aids must be monitored closely, and the results are seldom admissible in court.

Check your answers by comparing them with the summary of Chapter 6 in your text.

Chapter 7

IDENTIFYING AND ARRESTING SUSPECTS

_____

CHAPTER 7 QUESTIONS

Answer each question as completely as you can.

1.   What is field identification and when is it used?

2.   What rights does a suspect have during field identification and what case established these rights?

3.   How is a suspect developed?

4.   How can investigators help witnesses describe a suspect and/or a vehicle?

5.   When are mug shots used?

6.   What is the NCIC and how does it assist in criminal investigations?

7.   What are the four basic means of identifying a suspect?

8.   What does photographic identification require and when is it used?

9.   What does a lineup require and when is it used?

10.   What rights do suspects have regarding participation in a lineup and which cases established these rights?

11.   When is surveillance used and what are its objectives?

12.   What are the types of surveillance?

13.   When is wiretapping legal and what is the precedent case?

14.   What are the objectives of undercover assignments and what precautions should you take?

15.   What are the objectives of a raid?

16.   When are raids legal?

17.   What precautions should you take when conducting a raid?

18.   When can you make a lawful arrest?

19.   When must probable cause exist for believing that a suspect has committed a crime?

20.   What constitutes an arrest?

21.   When is force justified in making an arrest? How much force is justified?

Check your answers with those that follow.

CHAPTER 7 ANSWERS

1.   Field identification is on-the-scene identification of a suspect by a victim of a witness to a crime. Field identification must be made within minutes after the crime.

2.   *United States v Ash, Jr.* (1973) established that a suspect does *not* have the right to have counsel present at a field identification.

3.   Suspects are developed through the following means:
   - Information provided by victims, witnesses and other persons likely to know about the crime or the suspect.
   - Physical evidence left at the crime.
   - Psychological profiling.
   - Information in the files of other agencies.
   - Informants.

4.   Ask very specific questions and use identification diagram to assist witnesses in describing suspects and vehicles.

5.   Have victims and witnesses view mug shots in an attempt to identify a suspect you believe has a record.

6.   The FBI's National Crime Information Center (NCIC 2000) contains criminal fingerprint records and information on wanted criminals and stolen property, including vehicles and guns.

7.   Suspects can be identified through field identification, mug shots, photographic identification or lineups.

8.   Use photographic identification when you have a good idea of who committed the crime but the suspect is not in custody or when a fair lineup cannot be conducted. Tell witnesses they need not identify anyone from the photographs.

9.   Use lineup identification when a suspect is in custody. Use at least five individuals of comparable race, height, weight, age and general appearance. Ask all to perform the same actions or speak the same words. Instruct those viewing the lineup that they need not make an identification. Avoid having the same person make both photographic and lineup identification. If you do so, do not conduct both within a short time period.

10.   A suspect does not have a right to a lawyer if a photographic lineup is used (*United States v Ash, Jr.*). Suspects may refuse to participate in a lineup, but such refusal can be used against them in court (*Schmerber v California*). Suspects have a right to have an attorney present during a lineup (*Unites States v Wade*).

11.   Surveillance, undercover assignments and raids are used only when normal methods of continuing the investigation fail to produce results. The objective of surveillance is to obtain information about people, their associates and their activities that may help to solve the criminal case or to protect witnesses.

12.   The types of surveillance include stationary (fixed, plant or stakeout) and moving (tight or close, loose, rough, foot or vehicle).

13.   Electronic surveillance and wiretapping are considered forms of search and are therefore permitted only with probable cause and by court order (*Katz v United States*).

14.   The objectives of an undercover assignment may be to gain a person's confidence or to infiltrate an organization or group by using an assumed identity and to thereby obtain information or evidence connecting the subject with criminal activity. Precautions for undercover agents:
    - Write no notes the subject can read.
    - Carry no identification other than the cover ID.
    - Ensure that any communication with headquarters is covert.
    - Do not suggest, plan, initiate or participate in criminal activity.

15.   The objectives of a raid are to recover stolen property, seize evidence or arrest a suspect.

16.   A raid must be the result of a hot pursuit or be under the authority of a no-knock arrest or search warrant.

17.   Precautions when conducting raids:
- Ensure the raid is legal.
- Plan carefully.
- Assign adequate personnel and equipment.
- Thoroughly brief every member of the raiding party.
- Be aware of the possibility of surreptitious surveillance devices at the raid site.

18.   Police officers are authorized to make an arrest:
- For any crime committed in their presence.
- For a felony not committed in their presence if they have probable cause to believe the person committed the crime.
- Under the authority of an arrest warrant.

19.   Probable cause for believing the suspect committed a crime must be established before a lawful arrest can be made.

20.   If your intent is to make an arrest and you inform the suspect of this intent, then restrict the suspect's right to go free, you have made an arrest.

21.   When making an arrest, use only as much force as is necessary to overcome any resistance. If no resistance occurs, you may not use any force.

KEY TERMS

Define each term in the space provided.

arrest

bugging

close tail

cover

criminal profiling

electronic surveillance

entrapment

exceptional force

field identification

fixed surveillance

geographic profiling

lineup identification

loose tail

moving surveillance

National Crime Information Center (NCIC)

nightcap provision

photographic identification

plant

profiling

psychological profiling

raid

reasonable force

rough tail

solvability factors

stakeout

stationary surveillance

subject

surveillance

surveillant

tail

tight tail

undercover

wiretapping

Check your definitions by comparing them with those contained in the Glossary.

CHAPTER 7 SUMMARY

Fill in the blanks with the appropriate words and phrases.

Developing, locating, identifying and arresting _____ are primary responsibilities of

_____.

_____ _____ is on-the-scene identification of a suspect by a victim of or witness to a crime. _____ _____ must be made within minutes (usually 15 - 20 minutes) after a crime to be admissible. Suspects <u>do/do not</u> have the right to counsel at a field identification (*United States v Ash, Jr.*).

If the suspect is not immediately identified, you must develop a suspect through information provided by _____, _____ and other people likely to know about the crime or the suspect; through _____ _____ at the crime scene; through psychological _____; through information in _____ files; through information in other agencies' files; or through _____. Help witnesses describe suspects and vehicles by asking very _____ questions and using an _____ diagram.

Use the FBI's _____ _____ _____ _____ (NCIC 2000) to assist in developing or identifying suspects. The NCIC contains criminal _____ records and information on wanted criminals as well as on stolen _____ and _____.

Suspects can be identified through field identification, _____ shots, photographic identification or _____. Use field identification when the suspect is arrested at or near the scene. Use mug-shot identification if you believe the suspect has a _____ _____. Use _____ identification when you are reasonably sure who committed the crime but the suspect is not in custody or a fair lineup cannot be conducted. The pictures should portray at least _____ people of comparable race, height, weight and general appearance. Tell witnesses they need not identify anyone from the photographs. A suspect <u>does</u>/<u>does *not*</u> have the right to a lawyer if a photographic lineup is used (*United States v Ash, Jr.*).

Use _____ identification when the suspect is in custody. Have at least _____ people of comparable race, height, weight, age and general appearance. Ask them all to perform the same _____ or speak the same words. Instruct those viewing the lineup that they need not make an identification. Suspects may refuse to participate in a lineup, but such refusal may be used against them in court (*Schmerber v California*). Suspects have a right to have an _____ present during a lineup (*United States v Wade*). Avoid having the same person make both _____ and _____ identification. If you do so, do not conduct both within a short time period.

Some investigations reach a point after which no further progress can be made without using _____, undercover agents or a _____. Before taking any of these measures, you should exhaust all alternatives.

The objective of surveillance is to obtain information about _____ or their _____ and _____ that may help solve a criminal case or protect witnesses. Surveillance can be _____ (fixed, plant or stakeout) or _____ (tail or shadow). Moving surveillance can be rough, loose or close (tight) and done on foot or by vehicle. _____ surveillance and _____ are considered forms of search and therefore are permitted only with _____ _____ and by direct court order (*Katz v United States*).

The objective of an undercover assignment may be to gain a person's _____ or to infiltrate an organization or group by using an _____ _____ and to thereby obtain information or evidence connecting the subject with criminal activity. If you are working undercover, write no _____ the subject can read, carry no identification other than the cover ID, make sure any communication with headquarters is _____ and do not suggest, plan, initiate or participate in any _____ _____.

The objectives of a _____ are to recover stolen property, seize evidence or arrest a suspect. To be legal, a _____ must be the result of a hot pursuit or under authority of a _____-_____ arrest warrant or a search warrant. Precautions in conducting raids include ensuring the raid is _____, planning carefully, assigning adequate _____ and _____, thoroughly briefing every member of the raiding party and being aware of the possibility of _____ _____ devices at the raid site.

An _____ may occur at any point during an investigation. Police officers are authorized to make an arrest (1) for any _____ committed in their presence, (2) for a _____ not committed in their presence if they have probable cause to believe the person committed the crime or (3) under the authority of an _____ warrant. A lawful arrest requires that _____ _____ for believing the suspect committed a crime be established *before* the arrest.

If your intent is to make an _____ and you inform the suspect of this intent and then restrict the suspect's right to go free, you have made an _____. When making an arrest, use only as much force as is necessary to overcome any _____. If no _____ occurs, you may not use any force.

Check your answers by comparing them with the summary of Chapter 7 in your text.

Chapter 8

PREPARING FOR AND PRESENTING CASES IN COURT

CHAPTER 8 QUESTIONS

Answer each question as completely as you can.

1.   Why are some cases not prosecuted?

2.   How do you prepare a case for court?

3.   How do you review a case?

4.   What is included in the final report?

5.   What occurs during the pretrial conference?

6.   What is the usual sequence in a criminal trial?

7.   What is direct examination? What is cross-examination?

8.   What kinds of statements are inadmissible in court?

9.   How can investigators testify most effectively?

10.   When should notes be used while testifying?

11.   What nonverbal elements can influence courtroom testimony positively and negatively?

12.   What strategies can make testifying in court more effective?

13.   What defense attorney tactics should investigators anticipate?

14.   How can objections to your testimony be avoided?

Check your answers with those that follow.

CHAPTER 8 ANSWERS

1.   Cases are not prosecuted if:
- The complaint is invalid.
- The prosecutor declines after reviewing the case
- The complainant refuses to prosecute.
- The offender dies.
- The offender is in prison or out of the country and cannot be returned.
- No evidence or leads exist.

2.   To prepare a case for court:
- Review and evaluate all evidence, positive and negative.
- Review all reports on the case.
- Prepare witnesses.
- Write the final report.
- Hold a pretrial conference with the prosecutor.

3.   Concentrate on providing the elements of the crime and establishing the offender's identity.

4.   The final report contains (1) the complaint; (2) the preliminary investigation report; (3) all follow-up reports; (4) statements, admissions and confessions; (5) laboratory reports; (6) photographs, sketches and drawings; and (7) a summary of all negative evidence.

5.   At a pretrial conference with the prosecutor:
   - Review all the evidence.
   - Discuss the strengths and weaknesses of the case.
   - Discuss the probable line of questioning by the prosecutor and the defense.

6.   The sequence in a criminal trial is as follows:
   - Jury selection.
   - Opening statements by the prosecution and defense.
   - Presentation of the prosecutor's case.
   - Presentation of the defense's case.
   - Closing statements by the prosecution and the defense.
   - Instructions to the jury.
   - Jury deliberation to reach a verdict.
   - Reading of the verdict.
   - Acquittal or passing sentence.

7.   Direct examination is the initial questioning of the witness or defendant by the lawyer who is using the person's testimony to further his or her case. Cross-examination is questioning by the opposing side for the purpose of assessing the validity of the testimony.

8.   Inadmissible statements include:
   - Opinions and conclusions (unless the witness is qualified as an expert).
   - Hearsay.
   - Privileged communication.
   - Statements about character and reputation, including the defendant's criminal record.

9.   Guidelines for effective testimony:
   - Speak clearly, firmly and with expression.
   - Answer questions directly. Do *not* volunteer information.
   - Pause briefly before answering.
   - Refer to your notes if you do not recall exact details.
   - Admit calmly when you do not know and answer.
   - Admit any mistakes you make in testifying.
   - Avoid police jargon, sarcasm and humor.
   - Tell the complete truth as you know it.

10.   Refer to your notes if you are uncertain of specific facts, but do not rely on them exclusively.

11.   Important nonverbal elements include dress, eye contact, posture, gestures, distance, mannerisms, rate of speech and tone of voice.

12.   Rutledge's strategies for testifying in court include the following: (1) set yourself up, (2) provoke the defense into giving you a chance to explain, (3) be unconditional and (4) do not stall.

13.   During cross-examination the defense attorney might do the following:
    ▪ Be disarmingly friendly or intimidatingly rude.
    ▪ Attack your credibility and impartiality.
    ▪ Attack your investigative skills.
    ▪ Attempt to force contradictions or inconsistencies.
    ▪ Ask leading questions or deliberately misquote you.
    ▪ Ask for a simple answer to a complex question.
    ▪ Use rapid-fire questioning
    ▪ Use the silent treatment.

14.   To avoid objections to your testimony, avoid conclusions and nonresponsive answers. Answer yes-or-no questions with "yes" "no."

KEY TERMS

Define each term in the space provided.

cross-examination

direct examination

expert witness

magistrate

Check your definitions by comparing them with those contained in the Glossary.

CHAPTER 8 SUMMARY

Fill in the blanks with the appropriate words and phrases.

To prosecute or not to prosecute is often a question. Some cases are never prosecuted because the

complaint is _____, it is exceptionally cleared, or no _____ or leads exist. If

the decision is made to prosecute, thorough preparation is required. To prepare a case for court:

(1) review and evaluate all _____, positive and negative; (2) review all

_____ on the case; (3) prepare _____; (4) write the final _____; and

(5) hold a _____ conference with the prosecutor. Concentrate on proving the

_____ of the crime and establishing the offender's _____.

The final report contains (1) the _____; (2) the _____

investigation report; (3) all follow-up and progress reports; (4) _____, admissions

and _____; (5) _____ reports; (6) photographs, sketches and

_____; and (7) a summary of all _____ evidence. The quality of

the content and writing of the report influences its _____.

Before the trial, hold a conference with the prosecutor to review all the _____,

to discuss the _____ and _____ of the case and to discuss the probable

line of the prosecutors and defense attorney's _____.

A criminal trial begins with the _____ _____. When court convenes,

prosecution and defense make their _____ _____. The _____

then presents its case, followed by presentation of the _____ case. After closing

statements by the prosecution and the defense, the judge _____ the jury, which

then retires to deliberate its _____. When a _____ is reached, court is

reconvened and the verdict read. If the defendant is found _____, the judge passes

sentence or sets a sentencing date.

_____ examination is the initial questioning of a witness or defendant by

the lawyer who is using the person's testimony to further that lawyer's case. _____

examination is questioning by the opposing side with the intent of assessing the validity of the

testimony.

Certain types of statements are inadmissible in court, including _____,

conclusions, _____, _____ communications and statements about the

defendant's _____ and _____. To present testimony effectively speak

clearly, firmly and with _____; answer questions _____, and do/do _not_

volunteer information; _____ briefly before answering; refer to your _____

if you do not recall exact details; admit calmly when you do not know an answer; admit any

_____ you make in testifying; avoid police _____, sarcasm and _____;

and above all, tell the complete _____ as you know it. Refer to your notes if you

are uncertain of _____ _____, but do not rely on them excessively; this would

give the impression that you are not prepared for the case and thus weaken your testimony.

Important _____ elements include dress, eye contact, posture, gestures,

distance, mannerisms, rate of speech and tone of voice.

Strategies for testifying in court include (1) setting yourself up, (2) provoking the defense into giving you a chance to _____, (3) being _____ and (4) not _____. Anticipate the tactics commonly used by defense attorneys during cross-examination. They may be disarmingly _____ or intimidatingly _____; attack your _____ and impartiality; attack your investigative _____; attempt to force _____ or inconsistencies; ask leading questions or deliberately _____ you; request a "yes" or "no" answer to _____ questions; use _____-_____ questioning; or use the "silent treatment." To avoid objections to your testimony, avoid _____ and _____ answers. Answer yes-or-no questions with "yes" or "no."

If you are well prepared, know the _____ and present them truthfully and _____, you have done your part in furthering the cause of justice. The disposition of a case should be made known to the _____.

Check your answers by comparing them with the summary of Chapter 8 in your text.

Chapter 9

ROBBERY

CHAPTER 9 QUESTIONS

Answer each question as completely as you can.

1.   How is robbery defined?

2.   How are robberies classified?

3.   What are home invaders?

4.   In what types of robbery do the FBI and state officials become involved?

5.   What relatively new category of robbery has become a national concern?

6.   What are the elements of the crime of robbery?

7.   What special problems are posed by a robbery investigation?

8.   What factors should you consider in responding to a robbery-in-progress call?

9.   How can each element of robbery be proven?

10.   What descriptive information is needed to identify suspects and vehicles?

11.   What modus operandi information should you obtain in a robbery case?

12.   What physical evidence can link a suspect with a robbery?

Check your answers with those that follow.

CHAPTER 9 ANSWERS

1.   Robbery is the felonious taking of another's property, either directly from the person or in that person's presence, through force or intimidation.

2.   Robberies are classified as residential, commercial, street and vehicle driver.

3.   Home invaders are usually young Asian gang members who travel across the country robbing Asian families, especially Asian business owners.

4.   Bank robberies are within the jurisdictions of the FBI, the state and community in which the crime occurred and are jointly investigated.

5.   Carjacking, a relatively new category of robbery, is the taking of a motor vehicle by force or threat of force. It may be investigated by the FBI.

6.   The elements of the crime of robbery are:
   - The wrongful taking of personal property.
   - From the person or in the person's presence
   - Against the person's will by force or threat of force.

7.   The speed of a robbery, its potential for violence and the taking of hostages and the usual lack of evidence at the scene pose special challenges for investigators.

8.   When responding to a robbery-in-progress:
   - Proceed as rapidly as possible, but use extreme caution.
   - Assume the robber is at the scene unless otherwise advised.
   - Be prepared for gunfire.
   - Look for and immobilize any getaway vehicle you discover.
   - Avoid a hostage situation if possible.
   - Make an immediate arrest if the suspect is at the scene.

9.   Determine the legal owner of the property taken. Describe completely the property and its value. Record the exact words, gestures, motions or actions used to gain control of the property. Obtain a complete description of the robber's words, actions and any weapon used or threatened to be used.

10.   Obtain information about the suspect's general appearance, clothing, disguises, weapons and vehicles.

11.   Important modus operandi information includes:
- Type of robbery.
- Time (day and hour).
- Method of attack (real or threatened).
- Weapon.
- Number of robbers.
- Voice and words.
- Vehicles used.
- Peculiarities.
- Object sought.

12.   Physical evidence that can connect a suspect with a robbery includes fingerprints, shoe prints, tire prints, restraining devices, discarded garments, fibers and hairs, a note or stolen property.

KEY TERMS

Define each term in the space provided.

bait money

carjacking

robbery

Stockholm Syndrome

Check your definitions by comparing them with those contained in the Glossary.

CHAPTER 9 SUMMARY

Fill in the blanks with the appropriate words and phrases.

_____ is the felonious taking of another's property from his or her person or in his or her presence through force or intimidation. Robberies are classified as either _____, _____, street or _____-_____ robberies. One relatively new category is _____—the taking of a motor vehicle by force or threat of force. The _____ may investigate carjacking.

A relatively new type of residential robber is the _____ _____. Home invaders are usually young _____- gang members who travel across the country robbing _____ families, especially _____ business owners. The _____, state and _____ law enforcement personnel jointly investigate bank robberies.

The elements of robbery are (1) the wrongful taking of personal property, (2) from the person or in the person's presence, (3) against the person's will by force or threat of force.

The _____ of a robbery, its potential for _____ and the taking of _____ and the usual lack of _____ at the scene pose special problems. When responding to a robbery-in-progress call, proceed as _____ as possible but use extreme caution. Assume the _____ is at the scene unless otherwise advised, and be prepared for _____. Look for and immobilize any _____ _____ you discover. Avoid a _____ situation if possible, and make an immediate _____ if the situation warrants.

Prove each element of robbery _____. To prove that personal property was wrongfully taken, determine the _____ owner of the property and describe the property and its _____ completely. To prove that it was taken from the person or in the person's presence, record the exact _____, _____, _____ or actions

the robber used to gain control of the property. To prove the removal was against the victim's

will by force or threat of force, obtain a complete description of the robber's _____,

_____ and any _____ the robber used or threatened to use.

Obtain information about the suspect's general _____, _____,

disguises, weapon and _____ used. Important _____ _____

information includes type of robbery, time (day and hour), method of attack (threatened or

real), _____, object sought, number of _____, voice and words,

_____ and any peculiarities. Physical evidence that can connect the suspect with

the robbery includes _____, shoe prints, tire prints, _____ devices,

discarded _____, fibers and hairs, a note and the _____ property.

Check your answers by comparing them with the summary of Chapter 9 in your text.

Chapter 10

ASSAULT

CHAPTER 10 QUESTIONS

Answer each question as completely as you can.

1.   What constitutes assault?

2.   How does simple assault differ from aggravated assault?

3.   When is force legal?

4.   What are the elements of the crime of simple assault? Of aggravated (felonious) assault? Of attempted assault?

5.   What special challenges are posed in an assault investigation?

6.   How can the elements of both simple and aggravated assault be proven?

7.   What evidence is likely to be at the scene of an assault?

8.   What offenses might be categorized as separate crimes rather than simply as assault?

9.   What constitutes domestic violence?

10.   What constitutes stalking?

11.   What constitutes elder abuse?

Check your answers with those that follow.

CHAPTER 10 ANSWERS

1.   Assault is unlawfully threatening to harm another person, actually harming another person or attempting unsuccessfully to do so.

2.   Simple assault is intentionally causing another person to fear immediate bodily harm or death or intentionally inflicting or attempting to inflict bodily harm on the person. Aggravated (felonious) assault is an unlawful attack by one person on another to inflict sever bodily injury.

3.   In specified instances, teachers, people operating public conveyances and law enforcement officers can legally use reasonable physical force

4.   The elements of the crime of simple assault are:
   ▪ Intent to do bodily harm to another.
   ▪ Present ability to commit the act.
   ▪ Commission of an act toward carrying out the intention.

   An additional element of aggravated assault is that the intentionally inflicted bodily injury must have resulted in one of the following:
   ▪ A high probability of death.
   ▪ Serious, permanent disfigurement.
   ▪ Permanent or protracted loss or impairment of the function of any body member or organ or other severe bodily harm.

   Attempted assault requires proof of intent along with some overt act toward committing the crime.

5.   Special challenges in assault investigations include distinguishing the victim from the suspect, determining whether the matter is civil or criminal and determining whether the act was intentional or accidental. Obtaining a complaint against a simple assault also is sometimes difficult. Moreover, such calls may be dangerous for responding officers.

6.   To prove elements of assault, establish the intent to cause injury, the severity of the injury inflicted and whether a dangerous weapon was used.

7.   Physical evidence in an assault includes photographs of injuries, clothing of the victim or suspect, weapons, broken objects, bloodstains, hairs, fibers and other signs of an altercation.

8.   To aid in data collection, three special categories of assault are domestic violence, stalking and elder abuse.

9.   Domestic violence is defined as a pattern of behaviors involving physical, sexual, economic and emotional abuse, alone or in combination, by an intimate partner often for the purpose of establishing and maintaining power and control over the other partner (Geberth, 1998).

10.   Stalking generally refers to repeated harassing or threatening behavior.

11.   Elder abuse is the physical and emotional abuse, financial exploitation and general neglect of the elderly. The extent of elder abuse is currently unknown.

KEY TERMS

Define each term in the space provided.

aggravated assault

assault

battery

cyberstalking

domestic violence (DV)

elder abuse

felonious assault

in loco parentis

simple assault

stalker

stalking

Check your definitions by comparing them with those contained in the Glossary.

CHAPTER 10 SUMMARY

Fill in the blanks with the appropriate words and phrases.

_____ is unlawfully threatening to harm another person, actually harming another person or attempting unsuccessfully to do so. _____ _____ is intentionally causing another to fear immediate bodily harm or death or intentionally inflicting or attempting to inflict bodily harm on another. It is usually a _____. _____ assault is an unlawful attack by one person on another to inflict _____ bodily injury. It often involves use of a dangerous weapon and is a _____. In specified instances, _____, persons operating public _____ and law enforcement officers use physical force legally.

    The elements of the crime of simple assault are (1) _____ to do bodily harm to another, (2) present _____ to commit the act and (3) commission of an overt act toward carrying out the intent. An additional element in the crime of aggravated assault is that the intentionally inflicted bodily injury results in (1) a high probability of _____, (2) serious, permanent _____ or (3) permanent or protracted loss or impairment of the function of any body _____ or _____ or other severe bodily harm. Attempted assault requires proof of _____ and an _____ act toward committing the crime.

Special challenges in investigating assaults include distinguishing the _____ from the _____, determining whether the matter is _____ or _____ and whether the act was _____ or _____. Obtaining a complaint against simple assault is also sometimes difficult.

To prove the elements of the offense of assault, establish the _____ to cause injury, the _____ of the injury inflicted and determine whether a dangerous _____ was used. Physical evidence in an assault includes photographs of _____, _____ of the victim or suspect, _____, broken objects, _____, hairs, _____ and other signs of an altercation.

_____ assault, _____ and _____ abuse are candidates for categorization as separate crimes rather than being lumped in the general category of assault for reporting and research purposes. _____ violence is defined as a pattern of behaviors involving physical, sexual, economic and emotional abuse, alone or in combination, by an intimate partner often for the purpose of establishing and maintaining _____ and control over the other partner. _____ generally refers to repeated harassing or threatening behavior. _____ abuse is the physical and emotional abuse, financial exploitation and general neglect of the _____. The extent of elder abuse is currently

_____.

Check your answers by comparing them with the summary of Chapter 10 in your text.

Chapter 11

SEX OFFENSES

_____

CHAPTER 11 QUESTIONS

Answer each question as completely as you can.

1.   How are sex offenses classified?

2.   How is rape defined and classified?

3.   What are the elements of sexual assault?

4.   What modus operandi factors are important in investigating a sexual assault?

5.   What special challenges exist in investigating sex offenses?

6.   What is blind reporting and what are its advantages?

7.   What evidence is often obtained in sex offense investigations?

8.   What evidence should be sought in date rape cases?

9.   What agencies can assist in a sexual assault investigation?

10.   What is generally required to obtain a conviction in sexual assault cases?

11.   Have recent laws reduced or increased the penalties for sexual assault and why?

12.   Which three federal statutes form the basis for sex offender registries?

Check your answers with those that follow.

CHAPTER 11 ANSWERS

1.   Sex offenses include bigamy, child molestation, incest, indecent exposure, prostitution, rape (sexual assault) and sodomy.

2.   Forcible rape is sexual intercourse against a person's will by the use or threat of force. Statutory rape is sexual intercourse with a minor, with or without consent.

3.   The elements of sexual assault commonly include:
    - An act of sexual intercourse.
    - With a female other than the wife.
    - Committed without the victim's consent.
    - Against the victim's will and by force.

4.   Modus operandi factors important in investigating sex offenses include type of offense, words spoken, use of a weapon, actual method of attack, time of day, type of location and age of the victim.

5.   Special challenges to investigating rape include the sensitive nature of the offense, social attitudes and the victim'' horror and/or embarrassment. A rape investigation requires great sensitivity.

6.   Blind reporting allows sexual assault victims to retain their anonymity and confidentiality while sharing critical information with law enforcement. It also permits victims to gather legal information from law enforcement without having to commit immediately to an investigation.

7.   Evidence in a rape case consists of stained or torn clothing; scratches, bruises or cuts; evidence of a struggle and semen and bloodstains.

8.   Additional evidence in date rape cases may include the presence of drugs in the victim's system.

9.   A rape case often involves cooperation with medical personnel, social workers, rape crisis-center personnel and news media.

10.   Conviction in sexual assault cases requires medical evidence, physical evidence such as torn clothing, evidence of injuries and a complaint that is reported reasonably close to the time of the assault.

11.   Many recent laws have reduced the penalties for sexual assault, which should lead to more convictions.

12.   The evolution of sex offender registries can be traced to a trilogy of federal statutes: the Jacob Wetterling Act, Megan's Law and the Pam Lychner Act.

KEY TERMS

Define each term in the space provided.

bigamy

blind reporting

child molestation

cunnilingus

date rape

exhibitionist

fellatio

forcible rape

incest

indecent exposure

intimate parts

oral copulation

pedophile

penetration

prostitution

rape

Rohypnol

sadist

sadomasochistic abuse

sexual contact

sexual penetration

sexually explicit conduct

sodomy

statutory rape

voyeurism

Check your definitions by comparing them with those contained in the Glossary.

CHAPTER 11 SUMMARY

Fill in the blanks with the appropriate words and phrases.

Sex offenses include _____, child molestation, _____, indecent

exposure, _____, rape (_____ assault) and _____. The most

serious of these offenses is _____—sexual intercourse with a person against the person's

will. Rape is classified as _____ (by use or threats of force) or _____

(with a minor, with or without consent).

Most states include the following elements in defining the crime of rape or sexual

assault: (1) an act of _____ _____, (2) with a female other than the

_____, (3) committed without the victim's consent, (4) against the victim's will and by

_____.

Modus operandi factors important in investigating sex offenses include type of

_____, words spoken, use of a _____, method of attack, time of day, type of

_____ and _____ of the victim. Special challenges in investigating rape include the _____ nature of the offense, _____ attitudes and the victim's

_____. A rape investigation requires great _____. To help overcome

some of these challenges, many departments are implementing a procedure for victims of

sexual assault known as _____ _____, which allows sexual assault

victims to retain their anonymity and confidentiality while sharing critical information with law

enforcement. It also permits victims to gather legal information from law enforcement without

having to commit immediately to an _____.

Physical evidence commonly found in rape cases includes _____ or _____

clothing; _____, _____ and cuts; evidence of a _____ and _____

and bloodstains. Additional evidence in date rape cases may include the presence of _____

in the victim's system.

A rape case often involves cooperation with _____ personnel, _____

workers, rape crisis-center personnel and _____ _____. Conviction in sexual

assault cases requires _____ evidence, _____ evidence such as torn clothing,

evidence of _____ and a complaint that is reported reasonably close to the time of the

assault. Many recent laws have _____ the penalties for sexual assault, which

should lead to more _____.

The evolution of sex offender registries can be traced to a trilogy of federal statutes: the

_____ _____ Act, _____ Law and the _____ _____ Act.

Check your answers by comparing them with the summary of Chapter 11 in your text.

Chapter 12

CRIMES AGAINST CHILDREN

_____

CHAPTER 12 QUESTIONS

Answer each question as completely as you can.

1.   What crimes against children are frequently committed?

2.   What does the Child Protection Act involve?

3.   What effects can child abuse have?

4.   What challenges are involved in investigating crimes against children?

5.   When should a child be taken into protective custody?

6.   What factors should be considered in interviewing child victims?

7.   Are children generally truthful when talking about abuse?

8.   What is a multidisciplinary team?

9.   Who usually reports crimes against children?

10.   What types of evidence are important in child neglect or abuse cases?

11.   What things can indicate child neglect or abuse?

12.   What is a pedophile?

13.   What types of sex rings exist in the United States?

14.   How might a pedophile typically react to being discovered?

15.   How can crimes against children be prevented?

Check your answers with those that follow.

CHAPTER 12 ANSWERS

1. Crimes against children usually include kidnapping, abandonment, neglect, physical abuse, emotional abuse, incest and sexual assault.

2. The Child Protection Act (1984) prohibits child pornography and generally increases the penalties for adults who engage in it.

3. Child abuse can result in permanent serious physical, mental and emotional damage.

4. Challenges in investigating crimes against children include the need to protect the child from further harm, the possibility of parental involvement, the difficulty of interviewing children, credibility concerns and the need to collaborate with other agencies.

5. If the possibility of present or continued danger to the child exists, the child must be removed into protective custody.

6. When interviewing children, officers should consider the child's age, ability to describe what happened and the potential for retaliation by the suspect against a child who "tells."

7. In the vast majority of child abuse cases, children tell the truth to the best of their ability.

8. A multidisciplinary team (MDT) is a group of professionals who work together in a coordinated and collaborative manner to ensure an effective response to reports of child abuse and neglect.

9. Most reports of child neglect or abuse are made by third parties such as teachers, neighbors, siblings or parents. Seldom does the victim report the offense.

10. Evidence in child neglect or abuse cases includes the surroundings, the home conditions, clothing, bruises or other body injuries, the medical examination records and other observations.

11. Indicators of child abuse may be physical or behavioral both.

12. The pedophile is an adult who has either heterosexual or homosexual preferences for young boys or girls of a specific, limited age range.

13. Investigators should be aware of three types of sex rings: solo, transition and syndicated. Certain cults are also involved in the sexual abuse of children.

14. Pedophiles' reactions to being discovered usually begin with complete denial and then progress to minimizing the acts, justifying the acts and blaming victims. If all else fails, they may claim to be sick.

15.   Crimes against children can be prevented by educating them about potential danger and by keeping the channels of communication open.

KEY TERMS

Define each term in the space provided.

abandonment

"chicken hawk"

child sexual abuse

commercial exploitation

emotional abuse

exploitation

hebephile

kidnapping

lewdness

misoped

molestation

Münchausen Syndrome

Münchausen Syndrome by Proxy (MSBP)

neglect

Osteogenesis Imperfecta (OI)

physical abuse

sexual exploitation

sexual seduction

Sudden Infant Death Syndrome (SIDS)

temporary custody without hearing

visual medium

visual print

Check your definitions by comparing them with those contained in the Glossary.

CHAPTER 12 SUMMARY

Fill in the blanks with the appropriate words and phrases.

Crimes against children include _____, abandonment, _____,

exploitation, _____ abuse, _____ abuse, _____ and _____

assault. Such crimes can result in permanent and serious damage _____, mentally

and _____. The _____ _____ _____ prohibits child

pornography and greatly increases the penalties for adults who engage in it.

Challenges in investigating crimes against children include the need to protect the

child from further harm, the possibility of _____ involvement, the difficulty in

_____ children, _____ concerns and the need to collaborate

with other _____.

The primary responsibility of the responding officer is the _____ of the

child, and if the possibility of present or continued danger to the child exists, the child must be

placed in _____ _____. When interviewing children, officers should

consider the child's _____, ability to describe what happened and the potential for

_____ by the suspect against a child who "tells." In the vast majority of child abuse cases, children tell the _____ to the best of their ability. The current trend in investigating crimes against children is to use a _____ _____ (MDT), a group of professionals who work together in a coordinated and collaborative manner to ensure an effective response to reports of child abuse and neglect.

Most reports of child neglect or abuse are made by third parties such as _____, neighbors, _____ and _____. Seldom does the victim report the offense. When such reports are received, investigators must look for evidence of the crime, including the _____, the _____ conditions, clothing, _____ or other body injuries, the _____ examination report and other observations. Investigators should also listen carefully to children and should look for indicators of neglect or abuse. These indicators may be _____ or _____ or both.

Investigators should also be aware of _____—adults who have either heterosexual or homosexual preferences for young boys or girls of a specific, limited age range. Many pedophiles are members of _____ _____, three types of which have been identified: _____, _____ and _____. Certain _____ also practice sexual abuse of children. Pedophiles' reactions to being discovered usually begin with complete _____ and progress through _____ the acts, _____ the acts and _____ the victims. If all else fails, they may claim to be _____.

Crimes against children can be prevented by _____ them about potential dangers and by keeping the channels of _____ with them open.

Check your answers by comparing them with the summary of Chapter 12 in your text.

Chapter 13

HOMICIDE

CHAPTER 13 QUESTIONS

Answer each question as completely as you can.

1.   What is a basic requirement in a homicide investigation?

2.   What are the four categories of death?

3.   How are homicide, murder and manslaughter defined and classified?

4.   What degrees of murder are frequently specified?

5.   How do criminal and noncriminal homicide differ?

6.   How do excusable and justifiable homicide differ?

7.   What are the elements of each category of murder and manslaughter?

8.   What special challenges are encountered in a homicide investigation?

9.   What is first priority in a homicide investigation?

10.   How do investigators establish that death has occurred?

11.   How are unknown homicide victims identified?

12.   What factors help in estimating the time of death?

13.   What is cadaveric spasm and why is it important?

14.   What effect does water have on a dead body?

15.　　What are the most frequent causes of unnatural death and what indicates whether a death is a suicide or a homicide?

16.　　What information and evidence are obtained from a victim?

17.　　Why is determining a motive important in homicide investigations?

18.　　What physical evidence is usually found in homicides?

19.   What information is provided by the medical examiner or coroner?

Check your answers with those that follow.

CHAPTER 13 ANSWERS

1.   A basic requirement in a homicide investigation is to establish whether death was caused by a criminal action.

2.   The four types of death are natural, accidental, suicide and homicide.

Natural ⎤
Accidental ⎬— Noncriminal
Suicide ⎦

Homicide ——— Noncriminal or criminal

3.   Homicide is the killing of one person by another. It is classified as either criminal or noncriminal.

Murder is the unlawful killing of one person by another. It is classified as either first-, second- or third-degree murder.

Manslaughter is also the unlawful killing of one person by another but with no prior malice. It is classified as voluntary or involuntary.

4.   The three degrees of murder are specified as:

First degree	Premeditated and intentional, or while committing or attempting to commit a felony
Second degree	Intentional but not premeditated
Third degree	Neither intentional nor premeditated, but the result of an imminently dangerous act

5. Criminal and noncriminal homicide differ based on whether the act was felonious or not:

> Criminal (felonious)
>   Murder (first, second and third degree)
>   Manslaughter (voluntary and involuntary)
>
> Noncriminal (nonfelonious)
>   Excusable homicide
>   Justifiable homicide

6. Excusable homicide is the unintentional, truly accidental killing of another person. Justifiable homicide is killing another person under authorization of law.

7. The elements of each category or murder and manslaughter are as follows:

Element	Murder			Manslaughter	
	First Degree	Second Degree	Third Degree	Voluntary	Involuntary
Causing the death of another human	**	**	**	**	**
Premeditation	*				
Malicious intent	*	*			
Adequately provoked intent resulting in the heat of passion				*	
† While committing or attempting to commit a felony	*				
† While committing or attempting to commit a crime not a felony			*	*	
When forced or threatened				*	
Culpable negligence or depravity			*		
Negligence					*

† Indicates that the other single-starred elements need not be proven.

8. Challenges in homicide investigations include pressure by the media and the public, the difficulty of establishing that a crime has been committed, identifying the victim and establishing the cause and time of death.

9. The first priority is to give emergency aid to the victim if he or she is still alive or to determine that a death has occurred.

10. Signs of death include lack of breathing, lack of heartbeat, lack of flushing of the fingernail bed when pressure is applied to the nail and then released and failure of the eyelids to close after being gently lifted.

11.   Homicide victims are identified by family, relatives or acquaintances; personal effects, fingerprints, DNA analysis, dental and skeletal studies; clothing and laundry marks; or through missing-persons files.

12.   Factors that help in estimating the time of death are body temperature, rigor mortis, postmortem lividity (livor), appearance of eyes, stomach contents, stage of decomposition and evidence suggesting a change in the victim's normal routine.

        Body temperature drops 2 to 3 degrees in the first hour after death and 1 to 1 ½ degrees for each subsequent hour up to 18 hours.

        Rigor mortis appears in the head 5 to 6 hours after death; in the upper body after about 12 hours; and in the entire body after about 18 hours. After about 36 hours, rigor mortis usually disappears in the same sequence as it appeared.

        Postmortem lividity starts one-half to three hours after death and is congealed in the capillaries in four to five hours. Maximum lividity occurs within ten to twelve hours. The location of lividity can indicate whether a body was moved after death.

        A partial restriction of the pupil occurs in about seven hours. In twelve hours the cornea appears cloudy.

        The investigator should determine when and what the victim last ate. If any vomit is present, it should be preserved as evidence and submitted for examination.

13.   Cadaveric spasm is a sudden, involuntary tightening of muscles at the time of death. It occurs in specific muscle groups rather than the entire body and does not disappear as rigor mortis does. However, it does not occur in all deaths. Any weapon tightly clutched in the victim's hand as the result of cadaveric spasm indicates suicide rather than murder.

14.   A dead body usually sinks in water and remains immersed for eight to ten days in warm water or two to three weeks in cold water. It then rises to the surface unless restricted. The outer skin loosens in five to six days, and the nails separate in two to three weeks.

15.   Among the most common causes of unnatural death are gunshot wounds; stabbing and cutting wounds; blows from blunt instruments; asphyxia induced by choking, drowning, hanging, smothering, strangulation, gases or poisons; poisoning and drug overdoses; burning; explosions; electric shock; and lightning.

        In the case of a gunshot wound, suicide may be indicated if the gun was held against the skin, the wound is in the mouth or temple, the shot did not go through clothing or the weapon is present. Murder may be indicated if the gun was fired from more than a few inches away or from an angle or location that rules out self-infliction, if the victim was shot through clothing or if there is no weapon present.

Stabbing and cutting wounds may be the result of suicide if the body shows hesitation wounds; if the wounds appear under clothing or on the throat, wrist or ankles; if the weapon is present; or if the body has not been moved. Defense wounds, cuts through clothing or to vital organs, disfigurement, the absence of a weapon and signs that the body has been moved indicate murder.

Most cases of choking, drowning and smothering are accidental; most cases of hanging are suicide; most cases of strangulation are murder. Poisoning deaths can be accidental, suicide or murder. Most deaths caused by burning, explosions, electrocution and lightning are accidental, although burning is sometimes used in attempting to disguise murder.

16. The victim's background provides information about whether the death was an accident, suicide or homicide. If a homicide, the background often provides leads to a suspect. Evidence on the victim's body can also provide important leads.

17. Determine the motive for a killing because it provides leads to suspects and strong circumstantial evidence against a suspect.

18. Physical evidence in a homicide includes a weapon, a body, blood, hairs and fibers.

19. The medical examination or an autopsy provides legal evidence related to the cause and time of death and the presence of drugs or alcohol, and corroborates information obtained during the investigation.

KEY TERMS

Define each term in the space provided.

adipocere

asphyxiation

autoerotic asphyxiation

cadaveric spasm

criminal homicide

criminal negligence

defense wounds

excusable homicide

first-degree murder

heat of passion

hesitation wounds

homicide

involuntary manslaughter

justifiable homicide

lust murder

malicious intent

manslaughter

mass murder

mummification

murder

noncriminal homicide

postmortem lividity

premeditation

rigor mortis

second-degree murder

serial murder

suicide

suicide by police

third-degree murder

toxicology

voluntary manslaughter

Check your definitions by comparing them with those contained in the Glossary.

CHAPTER 13 SUMMARY

Fill in the blanks with the appropriate words and phrases.

Homicide investigations are _____ and frequently require all investigative

techniques and skills. A basic requirement is to establish whether death was _____ by

a _____ action. The four basic types of death are death by _____ causes,

_____ death, _____ and _____. Although technically you are concerned

only with _____, you frequently do not know at the start of an investigation what

type of death has occurred; therefore, any of the four types of death may require investigation.

Homicide—the killing of one person by another—is classified as _____

(felonious) or _____. _____ homicide includes murder and

manslaughter. _____ homicide includes _____ homicide—the

unintentional, truly accidental killing of another person—and _____ homicide—

killing another person under authorization of law. _____ is the essential element

of first-degree murder, distinguishing it from all other murder classifications.

Special challenges in homicide investigations include pressure by the _____ and

the _____, difficulty in establishing that it is homicide rather than _____ or an

accidental or natural death, identifying the _____ and establishing the _____

and _____ of death.

The first priority in a preliminary homicide investigation is to give emergency aid to the

_____ if he or she is still alive or to determine that _____ has occurred—

provided the suspect is not at the scene. Signs of death include lack of _____, lack

of _____, lack of flushing of the _____ _____ when pressure is applied

and then released and failure of the _____ to close after being gently lifted. After

priority matters are completed, the focus of the homicide investigation is to identify the

_____, establish the _____ of death and _____ of death and the

method used to produce it and to develop a _____.

Homicide victims are identified by their _____, friends or acquaintances; by

personal effects, _____, _____ analysis, skeletal studies including

_____, clothing and _____ marks; or through _____-persons files.

General factors used to estimate time of death are body _____, rigor

mortis, postmortem _____, appearance of the _____, _____ contents,

stage of _____ and evidence suggesting a change in the victim's normal routine. Body

temperature drops 2 to 3 degrees in the first _____ after death and 1 to 1½ degrees for

each subsequent hour up to _____ hours. _____ _____ appears in the head 5

to 6 hours after death; in the upper body after about 12 hours; and in the entire body after about ____ hours. After about _____ hours, rigor mortis usually disappears in the same sequence as it

appeared. Any weapon tightly clutched in the victim's hand as the result of _____ spasm

indicates _____ rather than _____. Postmortem _____ starts one-half

to three hours after death and is congealed in the capillaries in four to five hours. Maximum

lividity occurs within _____ to _____ hours. The _____ of lividity can

indicate whether a body was _____ after death. A partial restriction of the _____

occurs in about seven hours. In twelve hours the _____ appears cloudy. The investigator

should determine when and what the victim last _____. If any _____ is present,

it should be preserved as evidence and submitted for examination. A dead body usually _____

in water and remains immersed for eight to ten days in warm water or two to three weeks in

cold water. It then _____ to the surface unless restricted. The outer skin _____

in five to six days, and the _____ separate in two to three weeks.

Among the most common causes of unnatural death are _____ wounds;

_____ and cutting wounds; blows from _____ instruments; asphyxia induced by

_____, drowning, _____, smothering, _____, gases or poisons;

poisoning and _____ overdoses; burning; _____; electric shock; and

_____. In the case of a gunshot wound, _____ may be indicated if the

gun was held against the skin, the wound is in the _____ or _____, the shot did

not go through _____ or the _____ is present. _____ may be

indicated if the gun was fired from more than a few inches away or from an _____ or

location that rules out self-infliction, if the victim was shot through _____ or if there is

no _____ present. Stabbing and cutting wounds may be the result of suicide if the

body shows _____ wounds; if the wounds appear under clothing or on the

_____, _____ or _____; if the weapon is present; or if the body has

not been _____. Defense wounds, cuts through clothing or to vital organs,

disfigurement, the absence of a weapon and signs that the body has been moved indicate

_____. Most cases of choking, drowning and smothering are _____;

most cases of hanging are _____; most cases of strangulation are _____.

_____ deaths can be accidental, suicide or murder. Most deaths caused by burning,

explosions, electrocution and lightning are _____, although burning is sometimes used

in attempting to _____ murder.

The victim's _____ can also provide information about whether the death

was an accident, a suicide or homicide. This _____ and the _____ on

the victim's body often provide leads to a _____.

Determine a _____ for the killing to develop a suspect and to provide strong

_____ evidence against the suspect. _____ evidence in a homicide

includes a weapon, a body, blood, hairs and fibers.

A medical examination or an _____ provides legal evidence related to the _____

and _____ of death, and the presence of _____ or _____, and corroborates

information obtained during the investigation.

Check your answers by comparing them with the summary of Chapter 13 in your text.

Chapter 14

BURGLARY

_____

CHAPTER 14 QUESTIONS

Answer each question as completely as you can.

1.   How do investigators define *burglary*?

2.   What is the basic difference between burglary and robbery?

3.   What are the two basic classifications of burglary?

4.   What three elements are present in laws defining burglary?

5.   What additional elements can be included in burglary?

6.   What determines the severity of a burglary?

7.   What are the elements of the crime of possession of burglary tools?

8.   How should investigators proceed to a burglary scene, and what should they do on arrival?

9.   What special challenges are involved in burglary investigations?

10.   What is the most frequent means of entry to commit burglary?

11.   How are safes broken into, and what evidence should investigators look for?

12.   What physical evidence is often found at a burglary scene?

13.   What modus operandi factors are important in burglary?

14.   Where should investigators search for stolen property?

15.   What measure might be taken to prevent burglary?

Check your answers with those that follow.

CHAPTER 14 ANSWERS

1.   Burglary is the unlawful entry of a structure to commit a crime.

2.   Burglary differs from robbery in that burglars are covert, seeking to remain unseen, whereas robbers confront their victims directly. Burglary is a crime against property; robbery is a crime against a person.

3.   Burglaries are classified as residential or commercial.

4.   Elements of the crime of burglary include:
   - Entering a structure.
   - Without the consent of the person in possession.
   - With the intent to commit a crime.

5.   Elements of burglary can also include breaking into the dwelling of another during the nighttime.

6.   A burglary's severity is determined by the presence of dangerous devices in the burglar's possession or the value of the property stolen.

7.   Elements of the crime of possessing burglary tools include:
   - Possessing any device, explosive or other instrumentality.
   - With the intent to use or permit their use to commit burglary.

8.   Proceed to a burglary scene quietly. Be observant and cautious at the scene. Search the premises inside and outside for the burglar.

9.　　Special challenges in investigating burglary include false alarms, determination of the means of entry into a structure as well as into objects such as safes or vaults and recovery of the stolen property.

10.　　Jimmying is the most common method of entry to commit burglary.

11.　　Safes and vaults are entered illegally by punching, peeling, pulling, blowing, burning and chopping. Sometimes burglars simply haul the safe away.

12.　　Physical evidence at a burglary scene includes fingerprints, footprints, tire prints, tools, toolmarks, broken glass, safe insulation, paint chips and personal possessions.

13.　　Important modus operandi factors include time of day, type of victim, type of premises, point and means of entry, type of property taken and any peculiarities of the offense.

14.　　Check with fences, pawnshops, secondhand stores, flea markets and informants for leads in recovering stolen property.

15.　　Measures that deter burglaries include:
- Installing adequate locks, striker plates and door frames.
- Installing adequate indoor and outdoor lighting.
- Providing clearly visible addresses.
- Installing burglar-proof sidelight window glass beside doors.
- Installing a burglar alarm.

KEY TERMS

Define each term in the space provided.

blowing a safe

burglary

burning a safe

chopping a safe

commercial burglary

dragging a safe

fence

hit-and-run burglary

life style/exposure theory

peeling a safe

presumptive evidence

pulling a safe

punching a safe

residential burglary

routine activity theory

safe

smash and grab

vault

Check your definitions by comparing them with those contained in the Glossary.

CHAPTER 14 SUMMARY

Fill in the blanks with the appropriate words and phrases.

_____ is the unlawful entry of a structure to commit a crime. It differs from

robbery in that burglars are _____, seeking to remain unseen, whereas robbers

_____ their victims directly. Burglary is a crime against _____; robbery is

a crime against a _____.

     Burglaries are classified as _____ or _____. The elements of

the crime of burglary include (1) entering a _____ (2) without the consent of the

person in possession (3) with the _____ to commit a crime therein. Additional

elements of burglary that may be required include (1) breaking into (2) the dwelling of another

(3) during the _____. A burglary's severity is determined by the presence of

_____ devices in the burglar's possession or by the _____ of the

stolen property. _____ burglary and possession of burglary _____ are also

felonies. The elements of the crime of _____ burglary tools include (1) possessing

any device, explosive or other instrumentality (2) with intent to use or permit their use to

commit burglary.

When responding to a burglary call, proceed to the scene _____. Be observant

and _____. Search the premises inside and outside for the _____.

Special considerations in investigating burglary include the problem of _____ alarms,

determination of the means of _____ into a structure as well as into objects such as

_____ or _____ and recovery of the stolen property. _____ is

the most common method to enter a structure to commit burglary. Attacks on safes and vaults

include punching, _____, pulling or dragging, _____, burning, _____

and, for safes, hauling them away.

Physical evidence at a burglary scene often includes _____, footprints, tire

prints, _____, toolmarks, broken _____, safe _____, paint chips and

personal possessions. Important modus operandi factors include the _____, the types of

_____, the type of _____, point and means of _____, type of

_____ taken and any peculiarities of the offense.

Check with fences, _____, _____ stores, flea markets and

_____ for leads in recovering stolen property. Measures to deter burglaries

include installing adequate _____, striker plates and door frames; installing adequate

indoor and outdoor _____; providing clearly visible _____;

eliminating bushes or other obstructions to _____; securing any skylights or air

vents over 96 inches; installing burglar-proof _____ window glass beside doors;

and installing a _____ _____.

Check your answers by comparing them with the summary of Chapter 14 in your text.

Chapter 15

LARCENY/THEFT, FRAUD, WHITE-COLLAR AND ENVIRONMENTAL CRIME

CHAPTER 15 QUESTIONS

Answer each question as completely as you can.

1. How do investigators define *larceny/theft?*

2. How does larceny differ from burglary and robbery?

3. What are the elements of larceny/theft?

4. What are the two major categories of larceny and how are they determined?

5. What legally must be done with found property?

6.   What are the common types of larceny?

7.   When does the FBI become involved in a larceny/theft investigation?

8.   What are the elements of the offense of receiving stolen goods?

9.   What is fraud and how does it differ from larceny/theft?

10.   What are the common means of committing fraud?

11.   What are the common types of check fraud?

12.   What are the elements of the crime of larceny by credit card?

13.   What is white-collar crime, and what specific offenses are included in this crime category?

Check your answers with those that follow.

CHAPTER 15 ANSWERS

1.   Larceny/theft is the unlawful taking, carrying, leading or driving away of property from the possession of another.

2.   Both larceny and burglary are crimes against property, but larceny, unlike burglary, does not involve illegally entering a structure. Larceny differs from robbery in that no force or threat of force is involved.

3.   The elements of the crime larceny/theft are:
   - The felonious stealing, taking, carrying, leading or driving away
   - Of another's personal goods or property
   - Valued above (grand) or below (petty) a specified amount
   - With the intent to permanently deprive the owner of the property or goods.

4.   The categories of larceny/theft are grand larceny, a felony, and petty larceny, a misdemeanor—based on the value of the property stolen.

5.   In most states taking found property with the intent to keep or sell it is a crime.

6.   Common types of larceny are purse snatching, picking pockets, theft from coin machines, shoplifting, bicycle theft, theft from motor vehicles, theft from buildings, theft of motor vehicle accessories and jewelry theft. Altering the price of an item is considered larceny. It is not required that the person leave the premises with the stolen item before apprehension.

7. Always inform the FBI of jewel thefts, even without immediate evidence of interstate operation. Thefts of valuable art should be reported to the FBI and to INTERPOL, which also has an international stole art file.

8. The elements of the offense of receiving stolen goods are:
    ▪ Receiving, buying or concealing stolen goods.
    ▪ Knowing them to be stolen or otherwise illegally obtained.

9. Fraud is an intentional deception to cause a person to give up property or some lawful right. It differs from theft in that fraud uses deceit rather than stealth to obtain goods illegally.

10. Fraud is committed in many ways, including through the use of checks, credit cards, confidence games and embezzlement.

11. Common types of check fraud are insufficient-fund checks, issuing worthless checks and forgeries.

12. The elements of the crime of larceny by credit card include:
    ▪ Possessing a credit card obtained by theft or fraud
    ▪ By which services are obtained
    ▪ Through unauthorized signing of the cardholder's name

13. White-collar or business-related crime includes (1) securities theft and fraud, (2) insurance fraud, (3) credit-card fraud, (6) computer-related fraud, (7) embezzlement and pilferage, (8) bribes, kick-backs and payoffs and (9) receiving stolen property. Bank embezzlement is jointly investigated by the local police and the FBI.

KEY TERMS

Define each term in the space provided.

burls

confidence game

credit card

embezzlement

fence

flaggers

flipping

floor-release limit

forgery

fraud

goods

grand larceny

gray-collar crime

holder

larceny/theft

long-con games

petty larceny

poaching

property

shoplifting

short-con games

shrinkage

white-collar crime

zero floor release

Check your definitions by comparing them with those contained in the Glossary.

CHAPTER 15 SUMMARY

Fill in the blanks with the appropriate words and phrases.

_____ is the unlawful taking, carrying, leading or driving away of property from another's possession. It is synonymous with _____. Both larceny and burglary are crimes against _____, but larceny, unlike burglary, does not involve illegally entering a _____. Larceny also differs from robbery in that no _____ or threat of _____ is involved.

The elements of the crime of larceny/theft are (1) the felonious _____, taking, carrying, leading or _____ away of (2) another's personal _____ or _____ (3) valued above or below a specified amount (4) with the _____ to permanently deprive the owner of the property or goods. The two major categories of larceny/theft are _____ larceny—a felony based on the value of stolen property (usually more than $100)—and _____ larceny, a misdemeanor based on the value of the property (usually less than $100). In most states taking _____ property with the intent to keep or sell it is also a crime.

Among the common types of larceny are _____ snatching, picking _____, theft from _____ machines, _____, bicycle theft, theft from _____ _____, theft from _____, theft of motor vehicle _____ and _____ theft.

When dealing with shoplifters, remember that altering the price of an item is considered _____. Also remember that it is/is not usually required that a shoplifter leave the premises with the stolen item before apprehension. When investigating _____ theft, inform the FBI of the theft even if there is no immediate evidence of interstate operations. The elements of the offense of receiving stolen goods are (1) _____ , _____ or

_____ stolen or illegally obtained goods (2) _____ them to be stolen

or illegally obtained.

_____ is intentional deception to cause a person to give up property or

some lawful right. It differs from theft in that _____ uses _____ rather than

stealth to obtain goods illegally. _____ is committed in many ways, including through

the use of checks, credit cards, confidence games and embezzlement. Common types of check

fraud are insufficient-fund checks, issuance of _____ checks and _____ .

Elements of the crime of _____ by _____ _____ include

(1) possessing credit cards obtained by theft or fraud (2) by which services or goods are

obtained (3) through unauthorized signing of the cardholder's name.

White-collar or business-related crime includes (1) _____ theft and fraud,

(2) _____ fraud, (3) _____-_____ and check fraud, (4) consumer

fraud, illegal _____ and deceptive practices, (5) _____ fraud,

(6) computer-related fraud, (7) _____ and pilferage, (8) _____ , kick-

backs and _____ and (9) _____ stolen property. Bank embezzlements are

investigated jointly by the _____ police and the _____ .

Check your answers by comparing them with the summary of Chapter 15 in your text.

Chapter 16

MOTOR VEHICLE THEFT

_____

CHAPTER 16 QUESTIONS

Answer each question as completely as you can.

1.   What is a VIN is, and why is it important?

2.   What are the five major categories of motor vehicle theft?

3.   What are the elements of the crime of unauthorized use of a motor vehicle?

4.   What types of vehicles are considered "motor vehicles"?

5.   What is embezzlement of a motor vehicle?

6.   What is the Dyer Act, and how does it assist in motor vehicle theft investigation?

7.   Why are false reports of auto theft sometimes made?

8.   What two agencies can help investigate motor vehicle theft?

9.   How can investigators improve effectiveness in recognizing stolen vehicles?

10.   How can investigators help prevent motor vehicle theft?

Check your answers with those that follow.

CHAPTER 16 ANSWERS

1.   The vehicle identification number (VIN) is the primary nonduplicated, serialized number assigned by a manufacturer to each vehicle made. This number—critical in motor vehicle theft investigation—identifies the specific vehicle in question.

2.   Classifications of motor vehicle theft based on the motive of the offender include:
   - Joyriding.
   - Transportation.
   - Commission of another crime.
   - Stripping for parts and accessories.
   - Reselling for profit.

3.   The elements of the crime of unauthorized use of a motor vehicle are:
  - Intentionally taking or driving.
  - A motor vehicle.
  - Without the consent of the owner or the owner's authorized agent.

4.   Motor vehicles include automobiles, trucks, buses, motorcycles, snowmobiles, vans, self-propelled watercraft and aircraft.

5.   Motor vehicle embezzlement exists if the person who took the vehicle initially had consent and then exceeded the terms of that consent.

6.   The Dyer Act made interstate transportation of a stolen motor vehicle a federal crime and allowed for federal help in prosecuting such cases.

7.   False motor vehicle theft reports are often filed when a car has been taken by a family member or misplaced in a parking lot, when the driver wants to cover up for an accident or crime committed with the vehicle or when the driver wants to provide an alibi for being late.

8.   The FBI and the National Insurance Crime Bureau provide valuable help in investigating motor vehicle thefts.

9.   To improve you ability to recognize stolen vehicles:
  - Keep a list of stolen vehicles in your car.
  - Develop a checking system to rapidly determine whether a suspicious vehicle is stolen.
  - Learn the common characteristics of stolen vehicles and car thieves.
  - Take time to check suspicious persons and vehicles.
  - Learn how to question suspicious drivers and occupants.

10.   Numerous motor vehicle thefts can be prevented by effective educational campaigns and by installing antitheft devices in vehicles during manufacturing.

KEY TERMS

Define each term in the space provided.

chop shop

Dyer Act

keyless doors

motor vehicle

vehicle identification number (VIN)

Check your definitions by comparing them with those contained in the Glossary.

CHAPTER 16 SUMMARY

Fill in the blanks with the appropriate words and phrases.

Motor vehicle thefts take much investigative time, but they can provide important information on other crimes under investigation. The _____ _____ _____ (_____), critical in motor vehicle theft investigations, identifies the specific vehicle in question. This number is the primary nonduplicated, serialized number assigned by the _____ to each vehicle.

Categories for motor vehicle theft based on the offender's motive include (1) _____, (2) _____, (3) _____ for parts and accessories, (4) commission of another _____ and (5) _____ for profit.

Although referred to as "motor vehicle theft," most cases are prosecuted as "unauthorized use of a motor vehicle" because a charge of theft requires proof that the thief _____ to deprive the owner of the vehicle _____, which is often difficult or impossible to establish. The elements of the crime of unauthorized use of a motor vehicle are (1) _____ taking or driving (2) a motor vehicle (3) without the _____ of the owner or the owner's authorized agent. Motor vehicles include automobiles, _____, buses, _____, motor scooters, mopeds, _____, vans, self-propelled watercraft and _____. _____ of a motor vehicle occurs if the person who took the vehicle had consent initially and then exceeded the terms of that consent.

The _____ _____ made interstate transportation of a stolen motor vehicle a _____ crime and allowed for federal help in prosecuting such cases. _____ motor vehicle theft reports are often filed because a car has been taken by a family member or misplaced in a parking lot, to cover up for an _____ or a crime committed with the vehicle or to provide an _____ for being late. The _____ and the National _____ _____ _____ provide valuable help in investigating motor vehicle theft.

To improve your ability to recognize stolen vehicles, keep a list of stolen vehicles in your _____, develop a _____ _____ for rapidly determining whether a suspicious vehicle is stolen, learn the common _____ of stolen vehicles and car thieves, take time to check suspicious persons and vehicles and learn how to _____ suspicious drivers and occupants.

Numerous motor vehicle thefts can be prevented by effective _____ campaigns and by manufacturer-installed _____ devices.

Check your answers by comparing them with the summary of Chapter 16 in your text.

Chapter 17

ARSON

CHAPTER 17 QUESTIONS

Answer each question as completely as you can.

1. What is *arson*?

2. How are fires classified?

3. What presumption is made when investigating fires?

4. What are the elements of arson?

5. What constitutes aggravated arson? Simple arson?

6.   What degrees of arson are established by the Model Arson Law?

7.   Who is responsible for detecting arson? Investigating arson?

8.   What special challenges exist in investigating arson?

9.   What is the fire triangle, and why is it important in arson investigations?

10.   What are accelerants, and which are most commonly used in arson?

11.   What are common igniters used in arson?

12.   What are common burn indicators?

13.   How do investigators determine a fire's point of origin?

14.   How do fires normally burn?

15.   What factors indicate the likelihood of arson?

16.   When is an administrative warrant issued? A criminal warrant?

17.   When is a warrant needed for investigating a fire scene, and what is the precedent case?

18.   What should investigators check when investigating suspected arson of a vehicle?

19.   What should investigators pay special attention to when investigating explosions and bombings?

Check your answers with those that follow.

CHAPTER 17 ANSWERS

1.   Arson is the malicious, willful burning of a building or property.

2.   Fires are classified as natural, accidental, criminal (arson), suspicious or of unknown origin.

3.   Fires are presumed natural or accidental unless proven otherwise.

4.   The elements of the crime of arson include:
- Willful, malicious burning of a building.
- Of another, or of one's own to defraud.
- Or causing to be burned, or aiding, counseling or procuring such burning.

5.   Aggravated arson is intentionally destroying or damaging a dwelling or other property by means of fire or explosives or other infernal device—creating an imminent danger to life or great bodily harm, which risk was known or reasonably foreseeable to the suspect. Simple arson is an intentional destruction by fire or explosives that does not create imminent danger to life or risk or great bodily harm.

6.   The Model Arson Law divides arson into the following degrees:
- First-degree: burning of dwellings.
- Second-degree: burning of buildings other than dwellings.
- Third-degree: burning of other property.
- Fourth-degree: attempting to burn buildings or property.

7.   Logic suggests that the fire department should work to detect arson and determine the fire's point of origin and probable cause, whereas the police department should investigate arson and prepare the case for prosecution.

8.   Special challenges in investigating arson include:
- Coordinating efforts with the fire department and others.
- Determining whether a crime has in fact been committed.
- Finding physical evidence, most of which is destroyed by the fire.
- Finding witnesses.
- Determining whether the victim is a suspect.

9.   The fire triangle consists of three elements necessary for a substance to burn: air, fuel and heat. In arson one or more of these elements is usually present in abnormal amounts for the structure.

10.   Evidence of accelerants, substances that promotes combustion, especially gasoline, is a primary for of physical evidence at an arson scene.

11.   Common igniters include matches; candles; cigars; cigarettes; cigarette lighters; electrical, mechanical and chemical devices; and explosives.

12.   Common burn indicators include alligatoring, crazing, the depth of char, lines of demarcation, sagged furniture springs and spalling.

13.   The point of origin is established by finding the area with the deepest char, alligatoring and usually the greatest destruction. More than one point of origin indicates arson.

14.   Fires normally burn upward, not outward. They are drawn toward ventilation and follow fuel paths.

15.   Arson is likely in fires that:
- Have more than one point of origin.
- Deviate from normal burning patterns.
- Show evidence of trailers.
- Show evidence of having been accelerated.
- Produce odors or smoke of a color associated with substances not normally present at the scene.
- Indicate that an abnormal amount of air, fuel or heat was present.
- Reveal evidence of incendiary igniters at the point of origin.

16.   An administrative warrant is issued when it is necessary for a government agent to search the premises to determine the fire's cause and origin. A criminal warrant is issued on probable cause when the premises yield evidence of a crime.

17.   Entry to fight a fire requires no warrant. Once in the building, fire officials may remain a reasonable time to investigate the cause of the blaze. After this time an administrative warrant is needed, as established in *Michigan v Tyler* (1978).

18.   When investigating vehicle fires, look for evidence of accelerants and determine whether the vehicle was insured.

19.   When investigating explosions and bombings, pay special attention to fragments of the explosive device as well as to powder present at the scene. Determine motive.

KEY TERMS

Define each term in the space provided.

accelerants

administrative warrant

aggravated arson

alligatoring

arson

burn indicators

crazing

depth of char

fire triangle

igniters

line of demarcation

simple arson

spalling

strikers

trailer

Check your definitions by comparing them with those contained in the Glossary.

CHAPTER 17 SUMMARY

Fill in the blanks with the appropriate words and phrases.

Arson is the malicious, willful burning of a _____ or _____. Fires are classified

as natural, _____, criminal (_____), _____ or of unknown

origin. They are presumed _____ or _____ unless proven otherwise.

The elements of the crime of arson include (1) the _____, malicious burning

of a building or property (2) of another, or of one's own to _____ (3) or causing to

be burned, or aiding, counseling or procuring such burning. _____ arson is also a

crime. Some states categorize arson as either _____ or _____. _____

arson is intentionally destroying or damaging a dwelling or other property by means of fire or

explosives, creating an imminent danger to life or great bodily harm, which risk was known

or _____ _____ to the suspect. _____ arson is intentional

destruction by fire or explosives that does/does not create imminent danger to life or risk of

great bodily harm. Other states use the _____ _____ Law, which divides

arson into four degrees: first-degree involves the burning of _____; second-degree

involves the burning of _____ other than dwellings; third-degree involves the

burning of other _____; and fourth-degree involves _____ to burn

buildings or property.

Logic suggests that _____ departments should *detect* arson and determine the

_____ of _____ and probable cause, whereas _____ departments should

investigate arson and prepare cases for _____.

Special challenges in investigating arson include coordinating efforts with the _____ department and others, determining whether a _____ has been committed, finding _____ evidence and _____ and determining whether the victim is a _____.

Although the _____ department is responsible for establishing whether arson has occurred, law enforcement investigators must be able to verify such findings. To do so requires understanding the distinction between an _____ fire and _____. Basic to this understanding is the concept of the _____ _____, which consists of three elements necessary for a substance to burn: _____, _____ and _____. In arson, at least one of these elements is usually present in _____ amounts for the structure. Evidence of _____ at an arson scene is a primary form of evidence. The most common accelerant is _____. Also important as evidence are _____which include matches; _____; cigars and cigarettes; cigarette lighters; _____, mechanical and _____ devices; and _____.

Burn indicators that provide important information include _____, crazing, depth of _____, lines of _____, sagged furniture springs and _____. The point of origin is established by finding the area with the _____ _____, alligatoring and (usually) the greatest _____. Fires normally burn _____ and are drawn toward _____ and follow _____. Arson is likely in fires that:

- Have more than one _____ of _____.

- Deviate from normal burning _____.

- Show evidence of _____.

- Show evidence of having been _____.

- Produce _____ or smoke of a _____ associated with substances not normally present at the scene.

- Indicate that an abnormal amount of _____, _____ or _____ was present.

- Reveal evidence of incendiary _____ at the point of origin.

An _____ warrant is issued when it is necessary for a government agent to search the premises to determine the fire's cause and origin. A _____ warrant is issued on probable cause when the premises yield evidence of a crime. Entry to fight a fire requires no _____. Once in the building, fire officials may remain a reasonable time to investigate the cause of the blaze. After this time an administrative warrant is needed, as established in _____.

When investigating vehicle fires, look for evidence of _____ and determine whether the vehicle was _____. It is seldom arson if there is no _____. When investigating explosions and bombings, pay special attention to fragments of the explosive _____ as well as to _____ present at the scene. Determine _____.

Check your answers by comparing them with the summary of Chapter 17 in your text.

Chapter 18

COMPUTER CRIME

CHAPTER 18 QUESTIONS

Answer each question as completely as you can.

1.   What are the three key characteristics of computer crime?

2.   What can computer crime involve?

3.   What types of computer crime are most frequently committed?

4.   How should an investigator with a search warrant execute it in a computer crime investigation?

5.   How does evidence of computer crime differ from evidence of other felonies?

6.   What form does evidence usually take in computer crimes?

7.   What precautions should you take when handling computer disks?

8.   How should computer disks taken as evidence be stored?

9.   What approach is often required in investigating computer crime?

10.   Who is the "typical" suspect in a computer crime?

11.   What is the most frequent motive in such crimes?

12.   How can computer crimes be prevented?

Check your answers with those that follow.

CHAPTER 18 ANSWERS

1.
-   Computer crimes are relatively easy to commit and difficult to detect.
-   Most computer crimes are committed by "insiders".
-   Most computer crimes are not prosecuted.

2.   Computer crimes may involve the input data, the output data, the program, the hardware or computer time.

3.   The most common types of computer crime are misuse of computer services, program abuse and data abuse.

4.   Request the consent initially, and if that fails, use the search warrant—in that order.

5.   Computer evidence is often contained on disks, is not readily discernible and also is highly susceptible to destruction.

6.   Evidence is normally in the form of disks, data reports, programming or other printed information run from information in the computer.

7.   Avoid contact with the recording surfaces of computer disks. Never write on disk labels with a ballpoint pen or pencil or use paper clips or rubber bands with disks. To do so may destroy the data they contains.

8.   Store computer disks vertically, at approximately 70° F and away from strong light, dust and magnetic fields. Do not use plastic bags.

9.   Investigating computer crime often requires a team approach.

10.   Those involved in computer crimes are most commonly technical people such as data entry clerks, machine operators, programmers, systems analysts and hackers.

11.   Frequently motives for computer crimes are ignorance of proper professional conduct, misguided playfulness, personal gain and maliciousness or revenge.

12.   Computer crimes can be prevented by educating top management and employees and by instituting internal security precautions. Top management must make a commitment to defend against computer crime.

KEY TERMS

Define each term in the space provided.

boot

byte

computer crime

computer virus

cybercop

cybercrime

cyberpunk

cyberspace

disk drive

DOS

download

e-mail

floppy disk

gigabyte

hacker

hard disk

hardware

kilobyte

logic bomb

megabyte

modem

network

PC

piracy

program

scanner

script

software

trashing

Trojan horse

upload

virtual reality

Check your definitions by comparing them with those contained in the Glossary.

CHAPTER 18 SUMMARY

Fill in the blanks with the appropriate words and phrases.

Computer crimes are relatively easy to _____ and difficult to _____. Most computer crimes are committed by _____, and few are _____.

Computer crimes may involve _____ data, _____ data, the _____, the hardware or computer time. The most common types of computer crime are misuse of computer _____, _____ abuse and _____ abuse.

If investigators possess a search warrant and wish to conduct a search, they should first request _____ for the search. If consent is given, the search can proceed right away. If it is not given, then the _____ can be served and the search conducted.

Evidence in computer crimes is often contained on _____ or _____, is not readily discernible, and is highly susceptible to _____. In addition to information on disks or CDs, evidence may take the form of data reports, _____ or other printed materials based on information from computer files.

Investigators who handle computer disks should avoid contact with the _____ surfaces. Never write on computer disk labels with a _____ pen or _____ and never use _____ _____ on or _____ _____ around computer disks for to do so may destroy the data they contain. Computer disks taken as

evidence should be stored _____, at approximately _____ F and away from bright

light, _____ and _____ fields. CDs should be handled by their _____ and,

as with disks, kept away from extreme _____, direct _____, dust and

_____ fields.

Investigating such crimes often requires a _____ approach. Persons

involved in computer crimes are usually _____ people such as data entry clerks,

machine operators, _____, systems analysts and _____. Common

motivators for such crimes are _____, misguided _____, personal gain and

maliciousness or _____.

Computer crimes can be prevented by _____ top management and

employees and by instituting _____ _____ precautions.

Check your answers by comparing them with the summary of Chapter 18 in your text.

Chapter 19

ORGANIZED CRIME, GANG-RELATED CRIME, BIAS/HATE CRIME AND RITUALISTIC CRIME

CHAPTER 19 QUESTIONS

Answer each question as completely as you can.

1.   What are the distinctive traits of organized crime?

2.   What organized crime activities are specifically made crimes by law?

3.   What are the major activities of organized crime?

4.   What is the investigator's primary role in dealing with the organized crime problem?

5.   What agencies cooperate in investigating organized crime?

6.   What is a street gang?

7.   In what types of crimes do gangs typically engage?

8.   How are gang members identified?

9.   What kinds of records should be kept on gangs?

10.   What special challenges are involved in investigating illegal activities of gangs?

11.   What two defense strategies are commonly used by gang members' lawyers in court?

12.   What are bias or hate crimes?

13.   What is a cult?

14.   What is a ritualistic crime?

15.   What may be involved in cult or ritualistic crime?

16.   What are indicators of cult-related or ritualistic crimes?

17.   What special challenges are involved in investigating cult-related or ritualistic crimes?

Check your answers with those that follow.

CHAPTER 19 ANSWERS

1.   Distinctive traits of organized crime are:
- Definite organization and control.
- High-profit and continued-profit crimes.
- Singular control.
- Protection.

2.   It is a prosecutable conspiracy to:
- Acquire any enterprise with money obtained from illegal activity.
- Acquire, maintain, or control any enterprise by illegal means.
- Use any enterprise to conduct illegal activity.

3.   Organized crime is heavily involved in gambling, drugs, pornography, loan-sharking, money laundering, fraud and infiltration of legitimate business.

4.   The daily observations of local law enforcement officers provide vital information for investigating organized crime. Report all suspicious activities and persons possibly associated with organized crime to the appropriate person or agency.

5.   Organized-crime strike forces coordinate all federal organized crime activities and work closely with state, county and municipal law enforcement agencies.

6.   A street gang is a group of individuals who form an allegiance, have a name and recognizable symbol, claim geographic territory and engage in continuous unlawful or criminal activity.

7.   In addition to drug dealing, gang members often engage in vandalism, arson, shootings, stabbings, intimidation and other forms of violence.

8.   Gang members may be identified by their names, symbols (clothing and tattoos) and communication styles, including graffiti and sign language.

9.   Maintain records on gangs, gang members, monikers, photographs, vehicles and illegal activities. Cross-reference the records.

10.   Special challenges in investigating the illegal activities of gangs include the multitude of suspects and the unreliability or fear of witnesses.

11.   The two most often used defense strategies are pleas of diminished capacity and self-defense.

12.   Bias or hate crimes are motivated by bigotry and hatred against a specific group.

13.   A cult is a system of religious beliefs and rituals. It also refers to those who practice such beliefs.

14.   A ritualistic crime is an unlawful act committed with or during a ceremony. Investigate the crime, not the belief system.

15.   Ritualistic crimes are known to have included vandalism; destruction and theft of religious artifacts; desecration of cemeteries; the maiming, torturing and killing of animals or humans; and the sexual abuse of children.

16.   Indicators that criminal activity may be cult related include symbols, candles, makeshift altars, bones, cult-related books, swords, daggers and chalices.

17.   Special challenges involved in investigating ritualistic or cult-related crimes include separating the belief system from the illegal acts, the sensationalism that frequently accompanies such crimes and the "abnormal" personalities of some victims and suspects.

KEY TERMS

Define each term in the space provided.

Antichrist

Beelzebub

bias crime

Black Mass

Bloods

bookmaking

coven

Crips

cult

gang

graffiti

Hand of Glory

hate crime

incantation

loan-sharking

magick

money laundering

moniker

occult

organized crime

ritual

ritualistic crime

sabbat

street gang

swarming

turf

Check your definitions by comparing them with those contained in the Glossary.

CHAPTER 19 SUMMARY

Fill in the blanks with the appropriate words and phrases.

Distinctive characteristics of organized crime include definite _____ and control,

high-_____ and _____-profit crimes, _____ control and

_____. It is a prosecutable conspiracy to acquire any enterprise with money

obtained from illegal activity; to _____, _____ or _____ any

enterprise by illegal means; or to use any enterprise to conduct illegal activity. Organized crime

is continuously attempting to do all of the preceding with money obtained through its heavy

involvement in _____, drugs, _____, prostitution, loan-sharking, money

laundering, _____ and infiltration of _____ _____.

The _____ _____ of local law enforcement officers provide

vital information for investigating organized crime. All suspicious _____ and

_____ possibly associated with organized crime must be reported to the appropriate

person or agency. Organized-crime strike forces coordinate all _____ organized

crime activities and work closely with _____, _____ and _____

law enforcement agencies.

_____ to a gang is not illegal; however, the _____ of gang

members frequently *are* illegal. A _____ gang is a group of people who form an

alliance for a common _____ and engage in unlawful or criminal activity. In addition

to drug dealing, gang members often engage in _____, _____, _____,

_____, intimidation and other forms of violence. Gang members may be

identified by their _____, _____ (clothing and tattoos) and

_____ styles, including _____ and sign language. Maintain records

on gangs, gang members, _____, _____, _____ and illegal

activities. Cross-reference the records.

Special challenges in investigating the illegal activities of gangs include the multitude

of _____ and the unreliability or fear of _____. The two most often

used defense strategies are pleas of _____ _____ and _____-

_____.

Bias or hate crimes are motivated by _____ and _____ against a

specific group of people.

A _____ is a system of religious beliefs and rituals and those who practice them. A _____ crime is an unlawful act committed within the context of a ceremony. Investigate the _____—not the belief system.

Ritualistic crimes have included _____; destruction and theft of _____ artifacts; desecration of _____; the maiming, torturing and killing of _____ and _____; and the sexual abuse of _____. Indicators that criminal activity may be cult related include _____, _____, makeshift _____, _____, cult-related books, _____, daggers and _____. Special challenges in investigating ritualistic or cult-related crimes include separating the _____ _____ from the illegal acts, the _____ that frequently accompanies such crimes and the "abnormal" _____ sometimes found in both victims and suspects.

Check your answers by comparing them with the summary of Chapter 19 in your text.

Chapter 20

DRUG BUYERS AND SELLERS

_____

CHAPTER 20 QUESTIONS

Answer each question as completely as you can.

1.   How are drugs commonly classified?

2.   What drugs are most commonly observed on the street, in the possession of users and seized in drug raids, and what is the most frequent drug arrest?

3.   When is it illegal to use or sell narcotics or dangerous drugs and what physical evidence can prove these offenses?

4.   How can drug addicts be recognized? What are the common symptoms?

5.   What is the major legal evidence in prosecuting drug sale cases?

6.   When can an on-sight arrest be made for a drug buy?

7.   What precautions should be taken in undercover drug buys, and how to avoid a charge of entrapment?

8.   What hazards exist in raiding a clandestine drug laboratory?

9.   What agency provides unified leadership in combating illegal drug activities, and what is its primary emphasis?

Check your answers with those that follow.

CHAPTER 20 ANSWERS

1.   Drugs can be classified as depressants, stimulants, narcotics, hallucinogens, phencyclidine, cannabis or inhibitants.

2.   The most commonly observed drugs on the street, in possession of users and seized in drug raids are cocaine, codeine, crack, heroin, marijuana, morphine and opium. Arrest for possession or use of marijuana is the most frequent drug arrest.

3.   It is illegal to possess or use narcotics or dangerous drugs without a prescription and to sell or distribute then without a license.

4.   Common symptoms of drug abuse include:
  - Sudden, dramatic changes in discipline and job performance.
  - Unusual degree of activity or inactivity.
  - Sudden, irrational outbursts.
  - Significant deterioration in personal appearance.
  - Dilated pupils or wearing sunglasses at inappropriate times or places.
  - Needle marks or razor cuts or constant wearing of long sleeves to hide such marks.
  - Sudden attempts to borrow money or to steal.
  - Frequent association with known drug abusers or dealers.

5.   Physical evidence of possession or use of controlled substances includes the actual drugs, apparatus associated with their use, the suspect's appearance and behavior and urine and blood tests. The actual transfer of drugs from a seller to the buyer is the major legal evidence in prosecuting drug sale cases.

6.   If you observe what appears to be a drug buy, you can make a warrantless arrest if you have probable cause. Often, however, it is better to simply observe and gather information.

7.   Undercover drug buys are carefully planned, witnessed and conducted so that no charge of entrapment can be made. Make two or more buys to avoid the charge of entrapment.

8.   Clandestine drug laboratories present physical, chemical and toxic hazards to law enforcement officers engaged in raids on the premises.

9.   The Federal Drug Enforcement Administration (FDEA) provides unified leadership in attacking narcotics trafficking and drug abuse. Its emphasis is on the source and distribution of illicit drugs rather than on arresting abusers.

KEY TERMS

Define each term in the space provided.

crack

depressant

designer drugs

drug abuse

drug addict

excited delirium

flashroll

hallucinogen

mules

narcotic

sinsemilla

sting

tweaker

Check your definitions by comparing them with those contained in the Glossary.

CHAPTER 20 SUMMARY

Fill in the blanks with the appropriate words and phrases.

Drugs can be classified as _____, _____, _____,

_____, phencyclidine, cannabis or _____. The most common

drugs on the street, in possession of users and seized in drug raids are _____, opium,

_____, _____, _____, crack and _____. Arrest

for _____ or _____ of marijuana is the most frequent drug arrest.

It is illegal to possess or use narcotics or other dangerous drugs without a _____;

it is illegal to sell or distribute them without a _____. Investigators learn to recognize

drug addicts by knowing common symptoms of drug abuse, such as sudden, dramatic changes

in _____ or _____ _____; unusual degrees of _____

or _____; sudden, irrational _____; significant deterioration in personal

_____; _____ pupils or wearing sunglasses at inappropriate times or

places; _____ marks, _____ cuts or constant wearing of long sleeves to hide

such marks; sudden attempts to borrow _____ or to _____; and frequent

associations with known drug _____ or _____.

Physical evidence of possession or use of controlled substances includes the actual

_____, _____ associated with their use, the suspect's _____

and _____ and _____ and _____ tests.

Evidence of the actual _____ of drugs from the seller to the buyer is the

major _____ evidence required for prosecuting drug sale cases. If you observe what

appears to be a drug buy, you can make a _____ arrest if you have _____-

_____. Often, however, it is better simply to _____ and gather information.

Undercover drug buys are carefully planned, witnessed and conducted so that no charge of

_____ can be made. Two or more buys are made to avoid the charge of

_____.

Clandestine drug laboratories present _____, _____ and _____

hazards to law enforcement officers who raid them.

The _____ _____ _____ _____

(_____) provides unified leadership in attacking narcotics trafficking and drug abuse.

The _____'s emphasis is on the source and distribution of illicit drugs rather than on

arresting _____.

Check your answers by comparing them with the summary of Chapter 20 in your text.